LEBANON
NEW LIGHT IN AN ANCIENT LAND

By Elsa Marston

DILLON PRESS
New York

Maxwell Macmillan Canada
Toronto

Maxwell Macmillan International
New York   Oxford   Singapore   Sydney

For Salimi and Farid—"Teta" and "Jiddo"—
and all the Harik family

Photo Credits

Elsa Marston: cover, 8-9, 12, 23, 28, 33, 36, 50 (lower), 53, 56, 60, 64, 74, 81,
94, 96, 100-101; Ramsay Harik: 15, 25; Lebanon Tourist Council: 17, 20, 50
(upper), 73, 84; Imad Shweiry: 37; Nicholas Ghattas: 39; M. Maaiki: 58;
UNICEF: 104; Smithsonian Institution: 109, 111 113; St. Jude Children's
Research Hospital: 115; Westwood One Radio Networks/Casey Kasem: 116;
Donna Shalala: 118.

Library of Congress Cataloging-in-Publication Data

Marston, Esa.
    Lebanon : new light in an ancient land / by Elsa Marston.
      p. cm. — (Discovering our heritage)
    Includes bibliographical references and index.
    ISBN 0-87518-584-3
    1. Lebanon—Juvenile literature. [1. Lebanon.] I. Title. II. Series.
    DS80.M35   1994
    956.92—dc20   93-5402

Printed on recycled paper

Dillon Press
Macmillan Publishing Company
866 Third Avenue
New York, NY 10022

Maxwell Macmillan Canada, Inc.
1200 Eglinton Avenue East
Suite 200
Don Mills, Ontario M3C 3N1

Macmillan Publishing Company is part of the Maxwell Communication Group
of Companies.

First edition

10 9 8 7 6 5 4 3 2 1

Contents

Fast Facts about Lebanon

Official Name: Republic of Lebanon

Capital: Beirut

Location: Lebanon is situated in western Asia on the eastern shore of the Mediterranean Sea, bordered by Syria on the north and east, and Israel to the south.

Area: 4,015 square miles. Greatest distances are 135 miles long, 50 miles wide. Coastline, 130 miles.

Elevation: Highest, 10,138 feet. Lowest, sea level.

Climate: Mediterranean-type climate with hot, humid, but rainless summers, cool winters with rain. Highest mountains have snow eight months of the year. Average rainfall, 30 to 40 inches, about 50 inches in high altitudes, much less in Bekaa Valley. Temperature on the coast, 60° to 90°F in July, 35° to 50°F in January; about 15 degrees lower in mountains.

Population: Three million (estimate only, because of lack of census and recent migration and emigration).

Form of Government: Republic headed by a president, chosen by Parliament; deputies to Parliament elected by universal adult suffrage.

Important Products: Agriculture—wide variety of fruits, vegetables, grains; some tobacco; poultry. Industry—cement, energy production, oil refining, consumer products (plastics, textiles, ceramics, furniture, food processing, electrical appliances, etc.), service industry (banking, tourism).

Basic Unit of Money: Lebanese pound, also called lira.

Language: Official language is Arabic. The Armenian community speaks Armenian. Widespread use of English and French.

Religion: Estimates—50 percent Muslim, 40 percent Christian, 10 percent Druze. The largest single group are Shiite Muslims; Christians are divided among many sects.

Flag: Wide bands of red at top and bottom with a green cedar tree on a white band in the middle.

National Anthem: *Kulluna lil Watan* ("All of Us for the Homeland").

Major Holidays: Independence Day, November 22. New Year's Day. Muslim holidays: Ramadan, Aeed el Fitr, Aeed el Adha, Ashoura. Christian holidays: Christmas, Easter, Virgin Mary's Day.

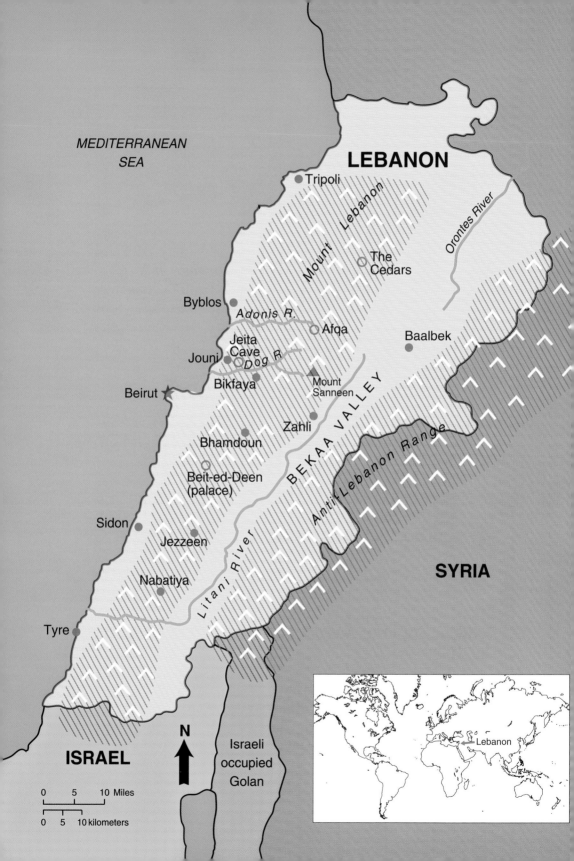

MEDITERRANEAN
SEA

LEBANON

● Tripoli

Mount Lebanon

Orontes River

○ The Cedars

Byblos ●

Adonis R.

○ Afqa

● Baalbek

Jeita
Cave
Jouni ○
Dog R.

Bikfaya ●

▲ Mount
Sanneen

Beirut ★

● Zahli

BEKAA VALLEY

Bhamdoun ●

Beit-ed-Deen ○
(palace)

Anti-Lebanon Range

Sidon ●

Jezzeen ●

SYRIA

Nabatiya ●

Litani River

Tyre ●

N

Israeli
occupied
Golan

ISRAEL

| 0 | 5 | 10 Miles |

| 0 | 5 | 10 kilometers |

Lebanon

1. Lebanon . . . The Land

Deserts, camels, and oil wells . . . that's the picture many people have of the Middle East. But Lebanon is different. This Middle Eastern nation is a land of mountains, trees, and water.

The size of Connecticut, one of our smallest states, Lebanon measures only 135 miles long and 50 miles at the widest. On the map it looks like a little patch between the Mediterranean Sea on the west, Syria on the north and east, and Israel on the south. Yet packed into that small space are enough natural beauty, history, and energy for several countries.

Snowcapped Mountains

The mountains and water have a lot to do with this. A mountain range runs the full length of the country, like a backbone. Since biblical times the range has been called "the Lebanon," or "Mount Lebanon." The word, from an ancient language of the area, means "white"—and indeed, the highest peaks are covered with snow for much of the year. The mountains reach their greatest height, a little over 10,000 feet, in the northern part of the country. The most beautiful peak, however—Mount Sanneen—is farther south and can be seen from Beirut, the capital city, on the coast.

To the east, a second mountain range runs parallel to the Lebanon range, along the border with Syria. Lower and more

Beirut, the capital of Lebanon, prior to the civil war. The city, built on a rocky peninsula, commands beautiful views of both mountains and sea.

barren, it is called the Anti-Lebanon. Between the two ranges
is a flat, fertile plain of rich reddish brown soil, about 5 to 10
miles wide. This is the Bekaa Valley.

Though the mountains are high and slashed by deep
gorges, many villages cling to their sides and ridges. Long
flights of stone steps run through villages built on steep slopes.
In a Lebanese village the very oldest houses are made of
yellowish stone, with walls up to three feet thick and flat roofs
covered with earth. Better houses have orange-tiled roofs,
which add to the color of the mountainsides. Stone is still used
for new buildings, but it is expensive. Most modern village
houses, therefore, are built of concrete and are not so attractive.
Old or new, houses are adorned with large rosebushes and
other flowers, which grow beautifully in the mountains.

Trees and Terraces

Wildflowers of many kinds cover the mountain slopes in the
spring. These rugged heights are striking in another way, too.
All over Lebanon, many of the mountainsides have been
carved into steps, called terraces. Some slopes have a hundred
or more terraces, each held up by a wall of rough stones. They
look like a giant's staircase. Today the terraces are filled with
fruit trees bearing the apples, cherries, peaches, plums, figs,
grapes, and other delicious fruits for which Lebanon is famous.
In their springtime bloom, the trees look like puffs of cloud
resting on the mountainside.

Years ago, villagers grew grains and vegetables on the
terraces. Living in remote places, with only the roughest of

roads, they had to produce most of their own food. Only by working hard to build and maintain the terraces could they manage to live in these high mountains.

The mountainsides are covered with pine trees. More famous, though, are the cedars. Long ago, these huge, stately trees grew over the whole mountain range. The Bible speaks of them, for they were beautiful and their wood greatly prized. But today, because of centuries of cutting—and herds of goats eating the seedlings—very few are left. A protected grove of about 400 fine old trees stands in one of the highest parts of the mountains. The image of the cedar, a symbol of eternal strength, appears on the national flag of Lebanon.

Sea, Snow, and Springs

Mountains, which give Lebanon its shape, also make possible the country's lifeblood—water. Clouds from the Mediterranean encounter the mountains and release the water they hold. Rain comes only in the cool months, from October through April, sometimes falling in torrents along the coast. In the high mountains, meanwhile, a thick blanket of snow builds up, which ensures that there will be enough water underground to feed the springs through the long, dry summer.

Some of the mountain springs are awesome, with hundreds or thousands of gallons of clear water gushing every minute. Wherever a good spring is found, there is almost certain to be a pleasant café nearby. A typical village spring, though, is small. The water comes through a pipe in a stone wall, where the villagers can drink or collect it in their jars. Traditionally,

Numerous villages, like this one called Dhour Shweir, dot the mountainsides.

the village spring, or "fountain," was a favorite place for neighbors to chat—and for young people to meet.

Lebanon's longest river, the Litani, flows 90 miles from the Bekaa Valley to the southern coast, and the Orontes River flows through the Bekaa in the other direction, north to Syria. Except in winter and spring, Lebanon's other streams are small. One, though, has created a spectacular sight, Jeita Cave. The river runs through the lower of the cave's two levels, and visitors see the cave and its strange formations by boat. The upper level contains a natural hall so huge, orchestra concerts have been given there.

Even with streams and springs, the Lebanese farmer must irrigate the crops and trees carefully. This is true not only in the mountains but also along the coastal plains, where citrus fruits and bananas grow, and on the vegetable and wheat farms of the Bekaa Valley. Fortunately the silver-green olive trees, which produce the olives and oil that Lebanese people like so much, can grow on their own.

Fresh water, plentiful compared with other Middle Eastern countries, keeps Lebanon green and beautiful. The salt waters of the sea have also been important in its history. The sea has invited people of Lebanon to explore the world, and, of course, it has brought other people to Lebanon.

Lebanon's largest port is at Beirut. In normal times the Beirut port receives goods from all over the world. Recently, the town of Jouni, which used to be a small, pretty village on a bay north of Beirut, has grown into a city with a busy port. The cities of Tripoli and Sidon also have ports. But the other great seaports of ancient times, Byblos and Tyre, now have little traffic other than local fishing and pleasure boating.

Beirut, Capital of Lebanon

Because the country is so small and most roads are fairly good, the farthest villages are only about a three or four hours' drive from Beirut. Beirut is the center of almost everything: transportation, government, education, medical treatment, business, banking. At least half the population of Lebanon live in Beirut and its suburbs.

Built on a rocky peninsula, the city has lovely views of both sea and mountains. A few fine old houses with orange-tiled roofs can still be seen among the modern, high-rise office and apartment buildings and hotels. In the recent past, Beirut was a bustling place. Both the boulevards and the many narrow, twisting streets were choked with cars, and the sidewalks teemed with people. Men pushing large carts of fruits and vegetables were also part of the street scene. Much of Beirut resembled a European city, with good restaurants, universities, movie theaters, and shops of all kinds.

A ring of poverty lay on its outskirts, however, mostly populated by people forced to leave their homes elsewhere. Also on the fringes of the city were many small factories.

In some ways this picture of Beirut is still true. But the long civil war that ravaged Lebanon in the 1970s and 1980s hit Beirut especially hard. The whole central part of the city, once the busiest part of all, was destroyed and has lain for many years a desolate wasteland. Likewise, the entire port area went up in smoke. No part of the city escaped fighting at one time or another.

Now efforts are getting under way to reconstruct totally the central city. A basic question is whether Beirut should be rebuilt along very modern, efficient lines, like a model city. Or should it somehow retain the jumbled but charming look of the past? The designers of the "new Beirut" face a difficult challenge.

Other Cities with Long Histories

On the northern coast is Lebanon's second largest city, Tripoli, which can be called the most traditional Muslim city in Lebanon. Its mosques and shops for Arabic sweets provide colorful contrast with high-rise buildings. Above the town is

Inside an Arabic sweet shop in Tripoli today

a castle built by European Crusaders in the 12th century, contrasting with the oil refineries along the waterfront.

Sidon and Tyre, on the southern coast, are also old cities, with many layers of history under their modern appearance. The first oil pipeline, built overland from Saudi Arabia in 1950, ends at Sidon. It had to cease functioning around 1985 because of the war. Both Sidon and Tyre suffered heavy damage during invasion by Israel in 1982.

Another coastal town is important in a different way. Byblos is one of the oldest continually lived-in towns in the world. Signs of human settlement there go back around 10,000 years. Its very ancient burials—along with Egyptian, Phoenician, Greek, Roman, Arab, and medieval European remains—make it a fascinating place to visit. On the other side of Mount Lebanon are two well-known towns. Zahli is a popular spot because of its many cafés along a rushing stream. Baalbek, in the Bekaa Valley, boasts some of the most spectacular Roman ruins in the world.

A Land of Villages, Too

Today Lebanon can be called an urban country. As many as 85 percent of the people live in or near cities and towns. This is a tremendous change in a short time, up from about 40 percent in 1960. At the same time, Lebanon is still a country of villages. Some are fairly large but are still thought of as villages. Though most people no longer live in the village their family originally came from, they still identify with and try to keep close ties with the place. That's the spot they love most.

The mountain villages are too cold in the winter for many people to live in them year-round. During the summer, however, when the coastal cities are hot and humid, everyone who can do so migrates to the mountains. If possible, people go back to their family villages for a few months. Cars, taxis, and buses rush constantly up and down the steep, winding roads. They take commuters down to jobs in the city and, in the afternoon, back to cool mountain homes. Some villages are popular summer resorts, attracting people from other parts of Lebanon and other countries, especially the oil-rich Arab states.

The People

The Lebanese people are almost all Arabs, with at most 10

The ancient city of Baalbek is famous for its Roman ruins.

percent of the population Armenian, plus a few Kurds. Typically, they have light tan or olive skin, black wavy hair, and large dark eyes. Some have very fair skin, and in the mountains one often sees faces that are quite ruddy. There are even some blonds, with blue or green eyes. A handsome people, the Lebanese are fond of Western ways and fashions.

The traditional costume of Lebanese men is no longer commonly seen but is still worn in some villages. It features an unusual type of black pants, very full and baggy from waist to knee and tight from knee to ankle. Formerly, a man wore a black jacket with fancy black trim stitched on it and, as a hat, a short, rounded cone of brown felt. These days, some village men wear the typical Arab head scarf called a keffiya, especially in the Bekaa and southern part of the country. The older men of a particular group called the Druze wear a coat of very tightly woven wool in colorful stripes.

Most women like Western styles, though some village women still wear long dresses. In the 19th century, well-to-do women dressed in very elaborate gowns of brocade and silk, with plenty of heavy jewelry. The young women of wealthy families in one part of the mountain also wore a tall, narrow silver cone on top of their heads, from which a veil fell gracefully.

Some Muslim Lebanese women recently have decided to cover their hair completely when in public. In this respect they are like women in other Muslim countries, where the custom of "covering" has been revived as a sign of religious belief. But more often, especially in the cities, Lebanese Muslim women dress as the Christian ones do—and they are very fashion-conscious.

Language

The language of Lebanon is Arabic. Written Arabic, a very old language, is the same throughout the Arab countries. A note at the end of this book describes the written language, also called classical Arabic. As for the spoken language, each country or region has its own variation. Small as Lebanon is, from one part of the country to another there are differences in the way people speak—and they love to make jokes about it.

In addition to knowing Arabic, everyone except those with very little schooling learns either French or English—and often both. Conversation tends to switch rapidly among the three languages. The Armenians living in Lebanon also speak their own language, Armenian.

Cultural Heritage

Because modern goods, both Lebanese-made and imported, are so plentiful, few people still practice old crafts. The Lebanese do, however, continue some traditional crafts such as silk brocade work and fine weaving, and the making of brassware, silver jewelry, colorful glassware, pottery, and carvings from olive wood. Table cutlery with bone handles carved in the shape of a bird is a famous specialty of a village called Jezzeen.

The 1960s and early 1970s brought a revival of folklore and arts. Folklore groups performed songs and dances in traditional costume, and new music was written combining Arabic with Western forms of music. During the war years, cultural events had to be greatly reduced, of course, but a few organizations still managed to encourage the arts and folk crafts. Books of high quality continued to be produced by some of Lebanon's many publishing houses, plus numerous magazines and journals. Now cultural and entertainment events, such as puppet shows for children and art exhibits, are once again available. Theater, especially the sort that pokes fun at government leaders and society, is very popular.

Lebanon's cultural heritage has suffered, however, in a serious way. Some of the ancient treasures of the Lebanese Museum disappeared early in the war years. Archaeological sites could not be protected. Whenever a rumor started that a

A potter in his workshop. Many traditional crafts are still practiced in Lebanon.

"treasure" of gold and silver had been found, people would start digging frantically at spots where they suspected there might be old ruins. Their response was partly understandable, as many people had become poor and desperate. But it has done a great deal of damage to some archaeological sites—damage that can never be repaired.

Lebanon has long been a cosmopolitan country, where people of many different religious, ethnic, and national groups live together. But since 1975, when the 16-year civil war started, Lebanon has been going through drastic changes. This book tries to describe Lebanon as it was in the recent past and as it is now. Although the deep wounds are starting to mend, only time can tell what shape Lebanon will take tomorrow.

2. The Lebanese Way—Getting Ahead

If the mountains are the backbone of Lebanon and its springs the lifeblood, then surely its people are the muscle. Although the Lebanese love to relax and enjoy life, what really stands out is their spirit of enterprise. The Lebanese are some of the world's best entrepreneurs—that is, people who start businesses and projects. They want to get ahead and they work hard for success.

A Nation of Entrepreneurs

For example, take building. In the 20 years before the recent war, large office buildings, luxury apartments, and hotels were going up almost overnight. It seemed as though nearly every square foot in Beirut would soon be built upon or paved over. Even during the war, while other parts of the country were being laid waste, the coast north of Beirut saw tremendous growth. And in the war-torn areas, people would get busy and start rebuilding as soon as they possibly could.

Whether they have a lot of money or very little, Lebanese entrepreneurs are always seeking new ideas for products and trade. For such a small country, with few natural resources, they manufacture a surprisingly large variety of products. Almost all are consumer goods, from cosmetics and cement to foods and furniture. There is a little heavy industry, such as production of machinery, but it has just started. Recently, high-tech recycling has become a profitable business.

The Lebanese had a huge "service industry" before the war. They were the bankers of the whole Middle East. Likewise, Beirut was the trading center of the region, with a port full of ships and constant traffic at Beirut International Airport. Hotels and entertainment served the many foreigners who came for business and other purposes. Probably much of this activity will be resumed before long.

Ambitious People

How did the Lebanese acquire so much "get-up-and-go"? Actually, even thousands of years ago the people who lived along the coast of what is now Lebanon were famous as successful traders. But perhaps it was especially their living in the mountains that encouraged the Lebanese people to work for themselves. For one thing, they had to work hard to make a living in that difficult terrain. Just as important, because they were rarely ruled by outsiders, the people of the mountains could lead their own lives. That gave them self-reliance and confidence. Then, in the 19th century, people in both the mountains and coastal cities started to become open to modern education and new ideas.

For a long time the Lebanese people have been known for their ambition. Though family members help one another, there are many "self-made" persons who succeed mainly through their own efforts. Some amazingly wealthy entre-preneurs started out with almost nothing but determination.

In war-torn Beirut, a determined man offers lemonade for sale.

And not just business executives! Whether a doctor, engineer, writer, or entertainer, a Lebanese person aims high.

The less educated and poorer people also want to improve their lives wherever possible. For instance, many farmers try new agricultural methods and crops. They are not resigned to the old ways, or willing to accept a poor life because "that's the way it has always been."

Those who don't get very far themselves usually want their children to do much better. It is often the mother who pushes the children, both girls and boys, to get a good education. Many people, even those with little education themselves, want their children to learn English well. English is used so widely all over the world that it is regarded as very important for getting a good job.

Besides leading to success in work, getting ahead is an everyday attitude as well. In shops everyone crowds around the counter, and the one with the loudest voice often gets served first. On the streets the drivers of taxis and *services* (cars that pick up and let off passengers along a certain route) all compete with one another. The faster they drive, the more trips they can make and the more money they will take in. Everyone else drives fast, too—and it seems as though everyone in Lebanon has a car.

In a discussion each person wants to get in his or her two cents worth. People don't *ask* for opinions or information—they *tell*. And they use lots of vigorous gestures to get their points across. Women have strong opinions and speak up almost as much as the men do. The Lebanese stand up for themselves.

Though Lebanese girls tend to be a little more shy than many American girls, today they are likely to be almost as ambitious and well educated as their brothers. They look forward to jobs in such fields as teaching, selling, and office work, and to careers in science, law, the arts, and all sorts of business. The demand for women's liberation has grown in recent years throughout the population.

Experts at Bargaining

The people of Lebanon would probably have a hard time getting things done if they did not also have skill in cooperating and "giving in" when necessary. Therefore, the Lebanese are some of the world's best bargainers. At a village shop, for example, a farmer may bring a crate of golden plums to the grocer. The shopkeeper offers a price, but the farmer wants more. As they haggle, women shoppers put in their views on the quality of the plums or the fairness of the price, until finally

Lebanese are skilled at bargaining—and they enjoy it. Here, on a busy street in Tripoli recently, shoppers negotiate with a nut seller.

the farmer and the shopkeeper manage to agree. Even for onlookers, bargaining is half the fun of buying and selling.

In the city three or four men may meet at an expensive restaurant to discuss a new partnership. Perhaps they want to process frozen orange juice, or start a new magazine or even a new bank. They enjoy the give-and-take of the planning. If their smartly dressed wives are present, the women are likely to add their opinions, too. But when the bill comes, the give-and-take ceases. Each man insists on the privilege of paying for everyone's lunch! Each wants to show traditional Arab hospitality and generosity . . . and also to assert himself.

Lebanon's Main Groups

Although the Lebanese know the importance of finding a good way out of any conflict, there are basic differences among them that sometimes make this very difficult. The people of Lebanon belong to many different religious groups. In some ways the history of Lebanon, past and recent, is the story of how these different groups have managed—and occasionally failed—to get along together. But it should be remembered that in spite of recent bitter conflicts, the people of Lebanon have lived together in peace much more than they have clashed.

Of the total population, which is probably now around three million, more than half are Muslim and a little less than half are Christian. No one knows the real figures or proportions, because no census has been taken since 1932. In any case, Lebanon is the only Middle Eastern country where the Christians constitute such a large and powerful part of the population.

Christians

Both Christians and Muslims are divided into different groups, called sects. There are at least 17 officially recognized sects. The largest Christian group is the Maronite Catholics. For many centuries they lived in the high mountains of northern Lebanon, and in the 18th and 19th centuries they moved to other parts of the mountain range. Of all the groups in Lebanon, the Maronites have traditionally thought of themselves as the most attached to an independent Lebanon, and some have felt that they were different from Arabs. Many are wealthy, and they have long been powerful in government, business, and education.

The Greek Orthodox people, the second largest Christian sect, live mostly in the coastal cities. Next in size are the Greek Catholics (also called Melkites). These religions are called Greek because they still use Greek language for some of their church services. Then come several smaller sects, including a few Protestants. All of these groups are about equally well educated, prosperous, and ambitious. On the whole, they share with the Muslims a feeling of Arab identity because they share language and culture with other Arab peoples.

Another large Christian group, whose members fled to Lebanon from Turkey early in this century, are the Armenians. Most live in and near Beirut. Armenians tend to be well educated and active in business and the professions, such as

An old Maronite Christian church in Mount Lebanon

teaching, medicine, and law.

There used to be a few thousand Lebanese Jews living in Beirut, but by the early 1980s nearly all had left the country.

Muslims

All Muslims follow the teachings of the Prophet Muhammad, who started the religion of Islam in the seventh century. There are, however, two main divisions among the Muslims. The Sunni Muslims could be called "mainstream." In Lebanon they have always lived in the coastal cities. Though Sunni Muslims favor strong ties with other Arab countries, they also value their Lebanese identity. Many are very prosperous and prominent in business, trade, education, and the professions.

Other Muslims, called Shiite or Shia, hold certain beliefs

about Islam that differ from those of the Sunnis. They form a distinct group and by now are the largest single sect in Lebanon. Since about 1980 the Shiite community has grown much stronger and better organized. There have long been educated city people among the Shiites, but in the past the majority were poor peasants in southern Lebanon and the Bekaa Valley. Large numbers had to leave their homes because of fighting in the south, starting in the 1970s, and now live in poverty in Beirut. For a long time the Shiites have been somewhat left out of Lebanon's prosperity. Now they want more power and recognition. They are loyal to Lebanon, but during the war some also came under the influence of the strong Shiite state of Iran.

Another sect, important even though small, are the Druze. Like the Christians they have lived in the mountains for many centuries. Though their religion originally came from Shiite Islam, it is kept secret from outsiders. A close-knit group, the Druze try to keep many of the old ways. They have a reputation as tough fighters, and at the same time are educated and enterprising.

There is another important group of people in Lebanon, which complicates the picture further. These are the Palestinian refugees, who were forced to leave their country in 1948 when it became Israel. Now about 350,000 Palestinians are living in Lebanon, though formerly their numbers were higher. Some, especially Christians, have become part of the life of the country and have even been given Lebanese citizenship. Most, however, have had to live all these years in special camps. They are nearly all Sunni Muslims. They do not want

to become part of Lebanon, for their goal is to have a
Palestinian state on territory that was once their country. For
people living in the refugee camps, "getting ahead" has been
very difficult indeed. In some ways they have been like a "state
within a state," and this has led to much trouble.

A promising change occurred in the fall of 1993: the start
of peace agreements between Palestinians and Israelis. The
future of the refugees is not yet clear, but with progress in the
creation of an autonomous, or independent, Palestinian state,
some refugees should be able to leave Lebanon and start new
lives in their own country.

Running Lebanon: Government

How do these different groups run the country together?
Lebanon has a democratic form of government. The citizens,
men and women, elect deputies to Parliament every four years.
In turn, the deputies choose a president for a six-year term. The
first elections in 20 years were held in September 1992. Some
Christians, however, were still uneasy and refused to vote.

The Lebanese system of government has an unusual
arrangement. Whereas in the United States religion and
government are supposed to be completely separate, in Lebanon
just the opposite is true. The government is organized according
to the strengths of the different religious sects. Formerly, the
Maronites were the largest sect, and therefore the president of
the Republic has always been a Maronite Christian. The prime
minister is a Sunni Muslim, and the Speaker of the House
(Parliament) is a Shiite. Other posts are distributed among

members of the various sects. This plan was agreed upon when Lebanon became independent in 1943, in the hope that no single group would dominate the others or be excluded.

In practice, however, the Christians—especially the Maronites—have had a lot of power through this arrangement, more than their numbers justify. The presidency is a strong office. Now that the Muslims have increased in importance and are the majority in the population, the system looks unfair to them. They want to change it. This has been a sore point in Lebanon for many years; in fact, it was one of the main reasons behind the recent war.

Besides the divisions among religious groups, wide differences exist between rich and poor. Although Lebanon has a strong middle class, such as people in business, education, and the professions, there are still very poor people. The needs of peasants in remote villages and city laborers have been neglected far too long. They need more of a chance to get ahead.

The determination of Lebanese people to prosper helps the whole country and enables most of the population to lead fairly comfortable lives. No less important, the spirit of enterprise encourages many freedoms in Lebanon. People may run for public office and vote freely. They may read what they choose and express opinions openly in Lebanon's dozens of newspapers. They can follow their religion freely and go into any line of work for which they can qualify. In making a strong country where these freedoms are protected and where they can live a good life together, the Lebanese will probably find that more unites than divides them.

3. Lebanon, 5,000 Years Old

Around 3,000 years ago, a powerful king died and was laid to rest. On his large stone sarcophagus were carved his name—Ahiram—and some other words. This was the first writing yet discovered in a form similar to what we use today: an alphabet. Therefore, the tomb of King Ahiram could be called the cradle of the alphabet!

The Phoenicians

The people whom Ahiram ruled were Phoenicians. At first known as Canaanites, they came to the shores of Lebanon from some place to the south around 3000 B.C. Much later the Greeks, who traded with them, gave them the name Phoenician. It comes from a word meaning "purple," because of the beautiful purple dye the Phoenicians made from a certain shellfish.

The Phoenicians lived in individual city-states along the coast. Each was ruled by a king with a council, which included wealthy merchants. The city of King Ahiram, Byblos, was one of the most important.

Besides developing a set of signs that stood for sounds and could be combined to make words, the Phoenicians left their mark in history in many ways. Never interested in war or conquest, they grew strong through trade. Probably their best

People have inhabited what is now Lebanon for thousands of years. The skeleton discovered in this burial site dates from around 5000 years ago.

customer was Egypt, to which they supplied cedarwood for the Egyptian temples, ships, and coffins. Skillful mariners, the Phoenicians discovered how to use the stars to plot a course across the waters. Their ships went around the coast of Africa and possibly as far as England.

Though the Phoenician cities were strong and rich, in time they lost their leadership in sea trade to the Greeks. Meanwhile, powerful rulers of nearby lands wanted to control this region, a crossroads between Asia and Africa and the Mediterranean. The Phoenician cities came to be ruled by Amorites, Egyptians, Hyksos, Assyrians, Babylonians, and Persians. Some of the conquerors even left "calling cards" that can be seen today. On the rocks where the Dog River meets the sea north of Beirut, foreign conquerors carved inscriptions showing that they had been there. Pharaoh Ramses II of Egypt seems to have been the first, around 1250 B.C., and his name was followed by many others—for more than 3,000 years. The last inscription in this unique record of history was left by the French, in 1946.

Greeks and Romans

A famous conqueror from Greece arrived in 334 B.C. Alexander the Great found the Phoenician cities of Byblos and Sidon willing to accept his rule. But the city of Tyre, which then was a well-defended island just off shore, resisted. Alexander built a roadlike causeway out to the island, brought his armies right up to the city walls, and finally overcame Tyre. The cities of Lebanon were ruled by Greeks for almost 300 years. They adopted many Greek ways, such as words, festivals, and architecture. Phoenicia itself, as a sort of nation, faded away.

Then along came mighty Rome. By 64 B.C. the whole region was under Roman rule. This brought growth and prosperity to Lebanon for about 600 years. The law school at the beautiful city Berytus (Beirut) was the most famous in the whole Roman world outside of Rome. Goods from the trading cities of Sidon and Tyre went everywhere, even to Britain. Well-built roads and bridges made travel easy within the country.

As the population grew, new villages and summer resorts sprang up in the mountains. For entertainment, people went to chariot races at the huge hippodrome in Tyre, to outdoor theaters, and to the "circus" to watch bloody fights. In the Bekaa Valley rose the amazing city of Heliopolis (Baalbek), with temples even larger and more beautiful than those in Rome. The columns of the Temple of Jupiter—six still stand today—were 62 feet high and 7½ feet in diameter.

In time the people of the area became Christian. After Rome was conquered in A.D. 476, the region was governed by the Eastern Romans, called Byzantines, from their capital at Constantinople (now Istanbul, Turkey). Gradually, however, this long, peaceful rule came to an end. Nature dealt a blow, too, destroying Berytus by earthquake, tidal wave, and fire in A.D. 551.

The Coming of Islam

The next century brought a lasting change for Lebanon. The

Arabs of the Arabian Peninsula were spreading rapidly
throughout the Middle East, bringing their new religion of
Islam. After years of fighting with Persian invaders, the
Byzantine rulers were weakened and the people discontented.
Cities on the Mediterranean coast accepted the new Arab

▲ *The few arches that remain of this 8th-century Arab palace give us an
idea of its grandeur and beauty.*

◄ *The columns of the Temple of Jupiter in Baalbek—62 feet high, 7½ feet
in diameter.*

rulers, and eventually the majority of the people also accepted the new religion and became Muslims.

The Arabs, desert and city dwellers, found the mountains too difficult to conquer. Some Christians held out in the remote heights of Mount Lebanon and were soon joined by another Christian group from Syria. These people came to be called Maronites, after an early leader named Maroun. The Maronites managed to stay relatively free of direct control for long periods of time and were allowed to live in their own way. On the whole, Lebanon prospered under Muslim rule and became known for its silk and other fine textiles.

Crusaders

In the late 11th century, Crusader knights from France, England, and other European countries set out for the countries of the eastern Mediterranean. Their main goal was to win Jerusalem and other places in the Holy Land from the Muslims. They also wanted the land and fabulous wealth of those countries.

After capturing Jerusalem in 1099 and killing its people, the Crusaders conquered the whole coast of Lebanon, Syria, and Palestine. Soon the land was carved up into separate small kingdoms, as in Europe. The Crusaders built castles, churches, and watchtowers, many of which can be seen today. For instance, in Lebanon there are impressive castles in Tripoli, Byblos, and Sidon, and a beautiful church, in daily use, in Byblos. The Crusaders' large, solidly built castles suggest that they expected to rule the Holy Land for a long, long time.

A castle built by the Crusaders still stands in Byblos.

Their stay lasted about 200 years. The Muslims gradually gained enough strength to fight back. The most famous Muslim leader, Saladin, fought against King Richard the Lion-Hearted of England in the late 12th century. Saladin is still known as both a skillful warrior and a wise, noble man. Bit by bit, the several Crusader kingdoms were overcome. By 1300 nothing remained of the Crusaders' dream of ruling the East.

The Europeans, nonetheless, made important gains from this contact between East and West. They learned about new foods and spices, and acquired many words from Arabic— even *sugar* and *candy*. Fine fabrics, carpets, mirrors, and other products of the area were soon in much demand. A new era of trade started.

As for the people of the East, they did not benefit nearly as much. Europeans at that time were far less civilized, learned, and scientific than the Arabs. The Crusaders left little behind them but blue-eyed descendants and castles—and one change among the people of Mount Lebanon. Some of the Christians, especially Maronites, had supported the Crusaders. This appears to have started contact between the Christians of Mount Lebanon and both France and the Catholic church of Rome.

For the next two centuries, beginning about 1300, military rulers from Egypt called Mamluks held power over Lebanon. It was a hard time, because the Mamluks were ruthless rulers. Earthquakes, plague, and famine added to the people's misery.

Ottoman Turks

Then new conquerors came, this time from the north. The Ottoman Turks, Muslims from Turkey, easily overran the Arab countries in 1516. The Turks ruled the coast and the Bekaa directly, but to a large degree they left the people of Mount Lebanon alone. As long as the Lebanese mountain chiefs, Druze and Christian, promised loyalty and certain payments, they were allowed to run their own affairs.

Around 1600 there arose a remarkable Lebanese leader. From an important family in Mount Lebanon, Fakhr-ed-Deen was a man small in size but great in ambition. He dreamed of creating a strong, independent kingdom.

With a well-trained army, Fakhr-ed-Deen gained control of a very large area—mountain, coast, and inland plains. Then he set out vigorously to modernize the country. He built good roads and bridges, and promoted agriculture and industry with the help of European advisers. Trade flourished; Italian princes and merchants were eager for all the Lebanese silk they could get. Fakhr-ed-Deen's rule was tolerant and fair toward all the religious groups, and the Christians prospered.

The Lebanese ruler's power and ever-growing military strength finally alarmed the Ottoman sultan. An army was sent against Lebanon. In 1635 Fakhr-ed-Deen was captured, taken to Constantinople, and executed. But he had opened the door to the future for Lebanon.

Ameer Basheer

After about 150 years another strong leader emerged. Basheer Shihab became ameer (prince) at age 21 and held power from 1788 to 1840. Dealing roughly with his rivals and with lawbreakers, Ameer Basheer brought all of Mount Lebanon under an orderly rule. His palace at Beit-ed-Deen is still one of the most splendid sights in Lebanon. Like Fakhr-ed-Deen, Basheer wanted to make Lebanon as independent from the Ottoman Turks as possible. He welcomed ideas and people from France and other European countries. American missionaries and teachers were also encouraged.

In 1831 the powerful ruler of Egypt, Muhammad Ali, came to Lebanon and Syria to fight against the Ottoman Turks. Basheer teamed up with him, and for a while the Egyptians controlled the whole area. They ran the country well at first, but then grew harsh. The people had to pay heavy taxes, serve in the army, and—what angered them most of all—give up their firearms.

The common people of the mountain rebelled in 1840. At the same time, Britain, Austria, and Ottoman Turkey got together to drive the Egyptians out of Lebanon and Syria. Ameer Basheer surrendered to the British and was exiled.

Time of Strife and Change

With his downfall, the traditional Lebanese government under a prince and local lords also came to an end. It had made the people of Mount Lebanon more free, safe, and prosperous than any other people in the Middle East. But now came a time of trouble.

The population had been increasing. In particular, the Maronite Christians were growing more powerful and were moving into parts of the mountain where they had not lived before. Christians and Druze became suspicious of each other and began to clash. Outside powers made matters worse. While France supported the Maronites, agents from Britain encouraged the Druze. The Turks, hoping to break down the existing system and gain control over Mount Lebanon themselves, favored the Muslims. In 1860 Druze and some Muslims attacked Christians on a wide scale, killing thousands and destroying villages.

The massacre of 1860 had one good result. Under pressure by European powers, the Ottomans set up a new form of self-government for Mount Lebanon, including a few of the smaller coastal towns. The wounds among the people healed over, though they were not forgotten.

Thanks to spreading education, Lebanon produced some writers and other intellectuals who sought change for the Arab countries under Ottoman rule. People began to demand not only reform but independence. When World War I broke out, however, the Ottoman Turks cracked down and took direct control of Mount Lebanon. Food supplies were stopped, people starved, and diseases spread.

The French Mandate

The Ottoman Empire ended with the Allied victory in 1918. After 400 years Lebanon was free of Turkish rule. But it was not free of foreign rule. The most powerful Allies, Britain and France, decided that the countries of the Middle East were not yet ready for full independence. A new system of government was tried, called the Mandates. The purpose was to keep these countries under the control of a European power for an indefinite time, while they became better prepared for self-government. France, because of its long ties with the Lebanese Christians, took charge of Mount Lebanon.

Under the French Mandate the major coastal cities and inland plain were added to the mountain, and the country acquired the shape it has today. Lebanon started to become a modern state. The French administrators favored the Maronite Christians, and French influence was very strong in education, government, and culture (language, ideas, styles). Though proclaimed a republic in 1926, Lebanon remained under French control. The Lebanese leaders and their people wanted full independence. During World War II, the French were persuaded, by pressure from both the Lebanese and the British, to end the Mandate. Lebanon became free in 1943, and the last French soldiers left its soil in 1946.

Independence—Prosperity and Problems

After independence Lebanon grew quickly as a center of trade, education, and communication between East and West. Its freedom and easy way of life attracted people from other Arab countries, Europe, and the United States. Business, banking, and building thrived.

Because of the differing views held by the several religious and political groups, however, uneasiness lay below the prosperity. In the mid-1950s the Lebanese president tried to tie his country too closely to the policies of the leading Western nations. This went against the strong pro-Arab feeling of at least half of the Lebanese people. Serious fighting broke out in 1958. The United States was asked to send marines, and did so, though they never took part in combat. The worst problems were settled in a few months. Under more careful leadership, the country was pulled together again.

Lebanon remains part of a much broader problem, however. In 1948 the whole Arab world was thrown into confusion by the establishment of Israel in what had been the Arab state of Palestine. Large numbers of Palestinians had to leave their homes and become refugees in neighboring Arab countries. Though Lebanon tried to stay out of military clashes between Israel and other Arab states, its people were naturally affected by the general unrest all around them.

The many Palestinians in Lebanon brought about a crisis. In the 1960s and 1970s, Palestinian fighters made attacks on Israel from bases in the south of Lebanon. Because of this, Lebanon came under Israeli attack. Shiite villages in the south were badly hit, and the people felt that the government was not doing enough to protect them. Some groups in Lebanon, mainly Muslim, supported the Palestinians, while some Christians, especially Maronites, opposed them. The careful balance between the different groups was breaking down.

The Long Civil War

War erupted in the summer of 1975. It started with small clashes between Maronite and Palestinian fighters, but it quickly involved many other groups, all with conflicting objectives.

The Muslims wanted an end to Christian-dominated government and a greater share of power and economic well-being. Dominant groups among the Christians wanted to hold on to all the power they had. Some Christians feared for their future in Lebanon if the Muslims, with the aid of the Palestinians, gained the upper hand. The Palestinian fighters wanted to carry on their struggle against Israel. The Syrians, who sent soldiers into the country in 1976 to stop the fighting, wanted to gain more political control over Lebanon. Israel wanted to get rid of the threat from Palestinians and have some control over Lebanon's policies and water resources. Meanwhile, the Lebanese people wanted to be left free to run their own country.

The first year of the war was especially terrible. Large parts of Beirut were destroyed, including the port area and the fashionable hotel district. The city became divided. Various fighting groups set up roadblocks in the parts of the city and the country that they controlled, which prevented people from moving from one area to another. Civilians, caught in the battles, suffered heavily. Tens of thousands were killed. Furthermore, many individuals were kidnapped and often killed by the different forces as a form of terrorism.

For a few years, with the Syrian army established in much of Lebanon, the conflict was less intense, but nothing was settled. Then in June 1982 Israel invaded Lebanon. Aiming at the Palestinian fighters in the south, Israeli armies destroyed large parts of Sidon and Tyre, and then attacked Beirut itself, causing great damage. Most of the Palestinian fighters were finally forced to leave the country, while some moved to bases in the Bekaa Valley.

Lebanon became divided among the fighting forces of Israelis, Syrians, Druze, Muslims, and Christians. A group of Shiite fighters took over the western part of Beirut.

Americans Get Involved

Meanwhile, an international peacekeeping force, including American marines, was trying to help the Lebanese army gain some control. Americans, supporting the Lebanese government, came under attack by groups who opposed the government. The U.S. Embassy was blown up by a car bomb in April 1983. In October of that year, a similar attack was made on the

U.S. Marine base near the Beirut airport, killing 241 Americans. The American forces, unable to help in the worsening conditions, were withdrawn in early spring of 1984.

Israel's army left Lebanon in the fall of 1983. United Nations troops continued to try to keep some sort of order in the southern part of the country, but they, too, suffered frequent attack.

Throughout the war the picture was extremely complicated because of the large number of different fighting groups. There were the armies of Lebanon, Syria, the Palestinians, and Israel, plus American and French forces and the United Nations. In addition, at least 19 different fighting forces, some large and some small, got into the fray. Called militias, these small armies fought with and against one another in what seemed a constantly changing lineup. It was like a football game in which all the players, for their own purposes, fight against all the other players, in some cases with outsiders calling the plays.

Several of the most important political leaders were assassinated. Although a new president was elected in September 1982, he could not provide leadership for such a splintered nation. Many people feared that Lebanon would have to be divided into at least two countries—or that it would be swallowed up by its neighbors. As the struggle continued through the 1980s, splits within the Christian side grew much worse. At one point there appeared to be two rival governments. Shiites, too, broke into two armies, which fought each other as well as the Palestinians.

In the mid-1980s there began another wave of kidnappings,

mostly by Shiite groups. This time about two dozen Americans and Europeans became victims. Some were held for several years as hostages, the last ones being released at the end of 1991.

With international pressure and mediation, many efforts were made to bring about a lasting cease-fire, but nothing took hold. Finally, in October 1989 an agreement was reached at a meeting held in Taif, Saudi Arabia. It provided for general principles and reforms for the governing of Lebanon. But the Taif Accord did not end the war. Intensely bitter fighting kept breaking out, mainly between some Christian forces who supported the accord and others who opposed both the accord and the powerful Syrian presence in Lebanon.

At last, in October 1990, the leader of the forces against the Taif Accord was overcome. Eventually the militias started to disband, and Lebanon began to experience peace in the spring of 1991—though still an uneasy peace. Syrian soldiers remained in control of much of the country, and Israel still held on to a strip in the south.

Results of the War

The price of those 16 years of fighting has been enormous. At least 120,000 people were killed and 300,000 wounded, most of them civilians. A great many people—something like 800,000—left the country, mostly the better-off and educated people. Within the country the population shifted around drastically. For example, the area north of Beirut became exclusively Christian, and parts of Beirut that used to have a lot of Christian people are now populated by Shiites. It is estimated that as many as 1,200,000 people had to move from their neighborhoods or regions—almost half of the entire population!

Though building and business boomed in certain areas controlled by the Christians, for the country as a whole the economy nearly collapsed. Businesses moved out or went bankrupt; people could not find work. Public morale suffered further because of the loss in value of the Lebanese money. For many years the value had been three Lebanese pounds to one U.S. dollar; but from 1984 on, the pound kept dropping until, early in 1993, it took nearly 2,000 pounds to equal one dollar. Though goods were plentiful, people had to have either dollars or piles of Lebanese pounds to buy anything. The rich became richer, and the poor became poorer.

The cost of rebuilding downtown Beirut alone is estimated at about $4 billion. All the cities and towns and many villages, even small, out-of-the-way ones, show heavy damage. In some areas a great many homes and other buildings have been nearly wrecked by soldiers of the Syrian and other armies living in them. The fighting forces and invading troops looted and destroyed much civilian property.

Nevertheless, in many ways life has now returned to normal. People can move around most of the country freely and meet their basic needs for food and goods. The national army, formerly split between different groups, is once again united and strong enough to keep the peace.

Now Lebanon must find ways to strengthen all its regions and all its different groups and classes of people. Many say

Emir Mansour mosque in downtown Beirut before the civil war . . .

. . . and after

that only by giving everyone a fair share in the country's prosperity can future violence be avoided. And only with a progressive government that has the support of all its people can Lebanon resist the pressures of outside powers. Lebanon will continue to be affected until the major conflicts in the region are settled, especially the one between Israel and the Palestinians. Fortunately, the peace negotiations between Israel and the Palestinians offer hope for a satisfactory outcome to that conflict within the next few years.

Somehow Lebanon has kept a special identity, often with an unusual amount of freedom, for most of its 5,000 years of history. Many people believe that its long history will go on, if the Lebanese can find their own way to bring unity and strength to their country once more.

4. The Lebanese at Home

In a traffic jam in Lebanon, or a lively discussion or a business deal, it's each one for himself. Or herself! But in other ways the group is more important than the individual. The family is most important of all. "If you don't have your family," a Lebanese person will say, "what have you got in life?"

Family members, including cousins and other relatives, help one another in education, business, and politics. They try to maintain the power and honor of the family. The individual member is expected to be loyal, do his or her share of helping, and go along with the interests of the family.

What is life like in a Lebanese home? Let's take a quick look at three different kinds of families.

A Rural Family

Many Shiite Muslim families, for example, live in small villages in the Bekaa Valley. Though some are tenant farmers and rent their land, the majority own their plots and raise small crops of wheat and vegetables. Their houses are built simply of stone or concrete with tile floors. There are only the most necessary pieces of furniture, very few decorations, and a small wood or kerosene stove for the winter.

These are large families. Ten to 15 children are not uncommon, partly because their help is needed for the farming.

A family gathering in a mountain village—"If you don't have your family, what have you got in life?"

The oldest daughters, after a few years of schooling, work in the fields or help their mothers. Formerly, girls met at the village spring every day and carried water home in a jar or large metal can, but now most houses have water. These days the favorite social center is the village bakery, the *foorn*. The girls and women go there to bake their homemade bread dough— and to catch up on the news.

Though some marriages are still arranged by families, girls now have a say in the matter. When a girl is married, she expects a life much like her mother's in some ways. She knows there'll be constant work—baking bread, washing clothes by hand, cooking and cleaning, preserving foods. She will probably have to do some work in the fields as well. But she wants a more comfortable life than her mother has had, a larger house and fewer children. *Her* daughters, she hopes, will finish secondary school and maybe get a job.

A Shiite girl is free to come and go in her own village, where everyone knows one another. But beyond that, her chances for fun and recreation may seem rather limited. If she is allowed to visit the nearby town of Zahli with her brothers, for instance, she may go to the shops—but probably not sit in a café.

For a boy in this Shiite village, life is more free than for his sister. When not working in the fields or doing his lessons, he may look for something a little mischievous to do with the other boys. But he must still be very careful not to do anything that would shame his family. People have strict ideas about honor and good behavior.

Many village boys today do not want to be farmers like their fathers. They want to go to secondary school in a nearby town, and someday get a good job in a factory or shop, or even an office job in Beirut. Better yet, go overseas and make a fortune!

Regardless of what the future may hold for him, a boy knows that his family rejoiced at his birth. When the first boy is born, from then on his parents are known not by their own names but as the mother and father of the boy. A woman is called, for example, Um Ahmed, meaning "Ahmed's mother," and a man is Abu Ahmed, "Ahmed's father." This is the custom among all Lebanese and other Arab people.

A Mountain Family

In a Christian family living in a mountain village, the mother may not have to work quite so hard as a woman in the more rural areas. She still has a full day. One job, for instance, that takes far more time in a village home than in most American homes is the laundry.

Even if the woman has a washing machine, it's most likely an old-fashioned one, and she will have to heat the water. She lights a fire under the water tank in the large tiled bathroom, using either packets of fuel or wood gathered from the mountain slopes. An hour later the water is hot and the machine can be filled. Then, when the week's clothes are washed, rinsed, and wrung out, the woman must hang them to dry. Up she climbs to the roof, if she has a flat one. There, among the grapevines that may be growing on the roof, she pins up the heavy, wet laundry. The whole job takes nearly all day.

A woman in a village family, whether Christian or Muslim, plays a strong role. Home life is valued highly by the Lebanese, and the woman who manages a home has an important job. She is respected and often has a forceful personality. Even so, these days her daughters will probably expect a different life, with higher education, possibly a job in Beirut—and certainly a better washing machine!

The sons of the family, when not in school, help their fathers with the gardens or orchards. (No housework for them!) There's always weeding, pruning, and spraying to be done. Mornings are for work, and afternoons bring visits with family and neighbors. In the early evening people take a stroll to the village square for ice cream and cakes at a café, or a movie.

In both village and city, girls live with their parents until

The flat roofs of modern Lebanese houses often serve many uses—a place to hang laundry, park a car, or practice some tennis.

they are married. Usually young men do, too. They are not eager to be on their own as soon as possible, and they accept their parents' authority, more or less willingly. When thoughts do turn to marriage, a Christian girl expects to choose her own husband, though she is guided by her family's views. Formerly, people thought a young man should choose a wife from the girls of his own village—and preferably a cousin. Now there is much more freedom.

A City Family

An educated family in Beirut or one of the other cities, regardless of religion, leads a life quite similar to those of many American families. It is quite acceptable, though not yet commonplace, for women to have careers.

But these families face difficulties, even with the larger incomes. Household help is hard to find and expensive; most helpers come from Sri Lanka these days. Living costs are very high, especially because the Lebanese money has lost so much value. An apartment with modern appliances costs a lot. So do good schools and music lessons for the children, a car, and nice clothes. Moreover, people in the world of business, government, and the professions are expected to lead a busy social life, with lots of parties and entertaining. It's not surprising that most educated couples want no more than two or three children.

In Beirut there are some families composed of a Muslim husband and a Christian wife. These would probably be well-educated people who don't want to be bound by traditional ways. Islamic law requires that the children of such a marriage be brought up as Muslims. (Marriage between a Christian man and a Muslim woman rarely happens, because it is forbidden by Islamic law.)

Lunch in a Village Home

The Lebanese, especially in villages, are courteous and friendly toward foreigners. If you visit a family, as a friend of one of their children, for instance, you will be very welcome. Arab hospitality is famous. Traditionally, the host must honor any guest—even an enemy—who enters his home.

Let's visit the summer home of a family—Druze, Christian, or Muslim—in the mountains. At the village square you will leave the bus or *service* car, and walk up the road to the house.

But stop for a moment! Here's something not seen very often anymore—a woman making bread in the old-fashioned way.

Seated on the ground outside her house, she lightly handles a ball of dough a little smaller than a baseball. Balancing a flat cushion on one arm, she starts tossing the dough from one arm to the other. With each toss the dough stretches more. It soon becomes a large circle about two feet across—and almost as thin as paper. Then the woman slaps the

dough from the cushion onto a circular piece of iron like a shallow dome, which rests over a small fire. It bakes in a few minutes. She peels the bread off and offers you a piece. Delicious! But don't eat too much, because there's a feast ahead at your friend's house.

Everyone in the family will come to meet you. "*Ahlan wa sahlan*," they will say, meaning "Welcome!" They will all ask, "How are you, how is your family?" But they probably won't ask more personal questions, about your background, for instance, or your interests. That would not be considered polite. The Lebanese expect people to say what they wish without being asked.

Your host will say, "*Beiti beitak*," meaning "My home is yours." This doesn't mean, though, that your hostess will let you "feel at home" by helping in some way. Arab hosts would not think of letting a guest work. You will sit and be served, and join the conversation the best you can. Any attempt you make to speak Arabic, even just a few words, will please your Lebanese friends enormously.

At about two in the afternoon, the lunch is ready. It is a banquet, for several pairs of hands have been working since early morning to prepare the food. There'll be *kibbe*—finely ground spiced lamb mixed with wheat and baked in a flat pan—and also *shish kebab*, cubes of meat broiled over a charcoal fire. You'll find *kefta*, too, which is ground meat mixed with finely chopped parsley, onions, and spices. Rice with pieces of chicken in a garlic-lemon sauce is another favorite dish. A neighbor has kindly brought over a whole tray of pastries stuffed with well-seasoned spinach, called *fatayer*.

Making bread the old-fashioned way

A Lebanese homemaker prepares pastries to be baked in the village foorn.

They're hot from the village *foorn*, where she took them to be baked.

No good meal is complete without *tabbouleh*, the ever-popular salad of chopped parsley, mint, tomatoes, onions, and wheat. With pieces of thin flat bread, everyone dips into *lebni*—thickened yogurt—and *hummus*, which is a paste made from chick-peas. *Baba ghannouj* is another dip, made from broiled eggplant. Lebanese food, one of the world's best styles of cooking, is not "hot" or unusually spicy, but it is *very* tasty.

The adults drink Lebanese beer and wine, or arak, a strong liquor that turns white when a little water is added. They call it "lion's milk." The young people can have something like Pepsi or Seven-Up, but they don't drink milk with meals.

For dessert the Lebanese usually enjoy their excellent

fresh fruits. There's also *baklava*—layers of paper-thin pastry with a filling of nuts, drenched with rosewater-flavored syrup. Another dessert, simple but delicious, is *muhallabiyya*, milk pudding.

And after Lunch . . .

The rest of the afternoon, after this huge "lunch," will be spent peacefully on the balcony, where the mountain scenery can be enjoyed. You will be offered a small cup of strong Arabic coffee. The backgammon board comes out, and so does the "hubbly-bubbly," the water pipe. This is a colorful contraption consisting of a large bottle of water and a long cord through which water-cooled smoke is puffed.

The young children are part of the group. Lebanese children have fewer toys and games than most American youngsters have, but they get lots of loving. All the family members and friends hug and kiss the little ones, and welcome older children affectionately as well. This probably helps Lebanese young people acquire their pleasant manners and self-confidence. In fact, you'll probably notice that Lebanese family members and friends are quite affectionate and touch one another a lot. Relatives, including men, may kiss one another on the cheeks, and friends often hold hands.

After a while some neighbors come. In village and city, visiting is usually of the drop-in variety, without plans or invitation. If the hosts are busy or already have guests, they still try to accept the newcomers graciously. Visiting is a very important part of village life. The usual hours for visits are from about four to eight o'clock. This doesn't conflict with dinner, however, because Lebanese families have a large midday meal and then a supper quite late.

Naturally it's sometimes hard for children to wait for supper when their parents have guests. But the Lebanese are fairly relaxed about bedtime hours—and everyone takes an afternoon nap when they have the chance. There's no napping on the day of your visit, of course . . . though everyone gets a little sleepy. When the conversation turns to politics, they all quickly wake up again.

By the time your friend walks with you down to the village square to get a *service* car back to Beirut, you have had a warm introduction to a Lebanese family. You can see how important the family is to all of its members.

Families in Wartime

During the war years, family life suffered. Large numbers of people left the country to escape the fighting, tension, and hardships, and to seek work elsewhere. Many parents who had to stay in Lebanon sent their children to the United States or Europe to school. Thus some families became very divided and scattered.

Other families lived through terrible years, lacking water, electricity, food, and fuel. They saw loved ones injured or killed, and endured endless days and nights of fear during the fighting. Though the Lebanese are quick to rebuild, some families will never have that chance.

On the other hand, some good things happened to families

in some cases. Many people left the city and returned to their villages. Long-parted family members were reunited and spent a lot of time together. People looked out for one another and helped one another emotionally.

It sometimes seems as though the family, like the religious group, may demand too much of a Lebanese person's loyalty. Although the future of Lebanon may require some change in that attitude, the family is truly one of the great strengths of the Lebanese people.

5. Holidays and Holy Days

In Lebanon it seems as though there's always a holiday coming up. Two main religions means twice as many holy days! Several are officially recognized, and everyone, whether a member of that religion or not, gets a day off from work or school.

Ramadan and Other Muslim Holy Days

The most important Muslim holy days last for a whole month, called Ramadan. This is the month of fasting, which starts when the new moon first appears. All day from sunrise to sunset, Muslims are supposed to go without food and drink. In the past, a cannon boomed at twilight to let people know when they could eat. Now it booms only on the radio. People still say to one another, as the sun sets, "It's almost cannon time." Then, losing no time, everyone sits down to a dinner as delicious as they can afford.

Before dawn a man walks through Muslim neighborhoods beating on a drum and reciting a religious poem. This wakes people up in time to have a good breakfast before fasting again.

Muslim festivals take place according to a calendar based on the phases of the moon, called the lunar calendar. Therefore,

During a recent festival in a Lebanese village, people enjoyed watching a traditional sword dance.

the dates change from year to year. This means that Ramadan sometimes comes in summer, when the long, hot days make fasting especially difficult.

Even so, Ramadan has a festive air. Mosques and Muslim neighborhoods are decorated with strings of lights. Shops that sell Arabic sweets do great business, and families budget their money to buy special treats for the nighttime meals. People visit one another a lot and have dinner and breakfast together. It's also a time for generosity and sharing with the less fortunate. Children, who usually do not fast before the age of about 11 or 12, look forward to the time when they may start, as a sign of growing up.

A big holiday comes at the end of Ramadan, when the new moon appears again. It is called the *Aeed el Fitr*, which means the "festival that breaks the fast." At this time the man comes around with his drum once more—to collect a tip for his services.

Fasting is a religious duty, but not every Muslim chooses to observe it. In any case, for most Muslims Ramadan is a high point of the year.

Another important Muslim festival is the *Aeed el Adha*, the Feast of the Sacrifice. It refers to the biblical story of Abraham, who prepared to sacrifice his son as proof of his devotion to God. Every village family who can afford it keeps a sheep for a few weeks, fattening it. In the cities sometimes sheep are kept on roofs and balconies, where they bleat day and night. The sheep is killed on the big feast day, and its meat often shared with poorer families.

The Feast of the Sacrifice is also a happy time, which goes

on for three or four days. Families visit, give presents, and wear new clothes. Swings for children are put up in public places. In the country, landowners sometimes give peasants money and clothes, and business people may do the same for their employees. Groups of boys and girls go out in the evening to enjoy the city streets.

A requirement of the Muslim religion, for all those who can fulfill it, is to visit the holy city of Mecca in Saudi Arabia. This is called the *hajj*, meaning "pilgrimage," which takes place during the Feast of the Sacrifice. When people return from the *hajj*, whole neighborhoods celebrate. Banners are stretched across the streets, welcoming the pilgrims and displaying verses from the Koran, the Muslims' holy book. Then, among family and friends, the pilgrims tell stories of their experiences. They may bring back delicious dates and special beads as gifts, plus little bottles of holy water from a certain well in Mecca.

Muslims also celebrate the Prophet Muhammad's birthday and Muhammad's ascent to heaven from Jerusalem. Both are days of rejoicing.

Islam appears to be a religion with much celebration of God's goodness. Its holidays bring fun for Muslim children, who eagerly await the gifts, clothes, and special treats. They look forward to visiting relatives, who are supposed to give them a little money. For poor families the holidays may be the only time they can afford new clothes. Noise is part of celebrating, too—not just fireworks, but gunfire. Even after years of warfare, many people, of all religions, still like to celebrate by shooting guns in the air.

A Shiite Holy Day

Shiite Muslims have an additional event, called the *Ashoura*, a very different kind of holy day. They observe the death of their religious hero Hussein, who was killed by treachery in the early days of Islam. The first ten days of the first month of the Muslim year are a time of mourning. People go to the mosque each night to pray and hear speeches. On the tenth day they take part in a procession. Men strike themselves lightly on the chest in rhythm to poems of grief, and a few may beat themselves with whips to show their sorrow. In Nabatiya, a town in southern Lebanon, a pageant is performed that re-creates the scene of the battle in which Hussein and his sons were killed. For the Shiites, therefore, the year starts off in mourning—but then gets better.

The Druze share one festival with the Muslims, the Feast of the Sacrifice, and they also celebrate the New Year on January 1. They have no other holy days, however, that are celebrated openly. The expression "on the festival of the Druze" means . . . "never"!

Christmas and New Year

One of the most enjoyable festival times, the Christmas and New Year's season, is almost a national holiday. Many Muslims also celebrate these holidays, although not in religious ways. For several weeks streets and shops are decorated with trimmings and lights. Shops are full for the gift-buyers. Churches hold bazaars, selling handcrafts and food.

On Christmas Day Christian families go visiting, particularly to honor the oldest members. Friends stop at one anothers' houses, and sugarcoated almonds are always offered. There's a big dinner at home, with turkey the traditional roast.

Lebanese people follow some Christmas customs learned from Americans and Europeans, starting with the missionaries who came in the 19th century. Some families have small Christmas trees, usually a scrawny type of cypress. Besides tinsel and ornaments, they may decorate the trees with homemade trims such as puffs of cotton and orange peels cut in fancy shapes. Though Santa Claus—often called Papa Noel—is becoming popular, Christmas is more a family festival than an occasion on which children expect to get lots of gifts.

New Year's Eve is celebrated equally by Christians and Muslims. Some city people go to parties and restaurants in their most elegant clothes. Otherwise, friends and families gather to have fun singing, joking, and dancing the national dance, called the *debki*. Many little customs are aimed at bringing good luck in the coming year. People play cards and games of chance, to see what kind of year lies ahead. A father gives his children some money as a sign that he hopes to provide well for his family all year.

In some families New Year's Day is more of a "gift day" than Christmas is. That's when children get the presents for which they have been hoping.

There used to be a special custom for Christ's Baptism Day, January 6. On this night, filled with magic and wonder for children, it was said that all the trees bowed down to Christ.

In the mountains people would go out in the morning to look for little marks in the snow where the trees had bent over.

Other Christian Holidays

For Lebanese Christians the Easter season has always been more important than Christmas. Palm Sunday is a special day for children, in memory of Christ's blessing the young at Jerusalem. Children dress in new spring clothes, some all in white. With their parents they parade around the church, carrying palm leaves, olive branches, flowers, and decorated candles as tall as themselves.

A traditional Easter ceremony takes place at midnight. Families go to the churchyard, holding candles. But they don't go into the church—for first the devil must be driven out. The priest bangs loudly on the closed door and calls, "Open the doors so the King of Glory can enter!" Inside the darkened church the "devil" answers, "Who is the King of Glory?" Twice more this is repeated. Then the doors burst open, the person playing the devil cries out and disappears, and all the lights go on. With church bells ringing, the people enter.

Easter is a time of rebirth. The mountains are covered with wildflowers, and the religious music is especially beautiful. Families have a large feast, including a special pastry called *ma'moul.*

And Easter eggs? Yes, indeed! The Lebanese custom—enjoyed by Muslims as well as Christians—is to dye boiled eggs at home using onion skins and certain wildflowers. Then families play a game with the colored eggs. Two persons hold their eggs tightly while one taps his or her egg against the tip of the other's, trying to crack it. The last egg to crack is the winner. It's not unknown for an egg to be secretly filled with candle wax to make it unbeatable!

Different Christian villages are known for celebrating particular saints. On the saint's day all the church bells in the area ring. In old mountain churches they are rung by pulling on a long rope that hangs down the outside of the building. Boys compete to see who can ring longest and jump the highest.

On August 15 comes the Virgin Mary's Day, when all churches named for Saint Mary have festivals. The best-known is in a large mountain town called Bhamdun. In the churchyard a thick stew of lamb and wheat cooks all night in big kettles. Church members take turns stirring it and keeping the fires going. When it is finally done, it is served to one and all as a symbol of God's goodness. And there are all the other things that make a festival: games, sweets, souvenirs—and fireworks. Fireworks, like bell ringing and gun shooting, are enjoyed on every possible occasion.

The Day of the Cross honors Saint Helena, mother of Constantine, the Roman emperor who adopted Christianity in the fourth century. According to legend, Helena journeyed to Jerusalem and found the remains of the cross on which Jesus was crucified. The good news was relayed back to Constantinople by bonfires lit on hilltops and mountains.

What a good excuse for a huge bonfire! Village children gather sticks and brush to make bonfires in front of their houses. On the night of September 13, the piles are set ablaze, and fires twinkle over the slopes of Mount Lebanon.

The Lebanese also have a day like Halloween—but this, too, is a saint's day, not a night for assorted spooks. Saint Barbara was an early Christian who had to disguise herself to escape from people who were pursuing her. On Saint Barbara's Day, December 4, young people used to dress up in masks and costumes and go around the neighborhood. At each house they would do a dance and sing a "treat or trick" song, accompanied by a small drum.

National Holidays and Festivals

The Lebanese observe some national holidays, too. Independence Day, November 22, celebrates Lebanon's receiving complete freedom from French rule in 1943. There are speeches, parades, flags. Martyrs' Day, in May, honors patriots who were executed by the Turks at the time of World War I.

Until the outbreak of fighting in 1975, Lebanon also had some festivals just for art and fun. One was the Flower Festival in the mountain town of Bikfaya. A parade with rose-covered floats and marching bands went through the town. People came from all over Lebanon to admire the flower decorations and enjoy the fun.

A famous international festival of music and drama was held for several years in the ruins of Baalbek. The columns and steps of the Roman temples made a spectacular stage setting. Excellent ballet, theater, and musical groups from many countries—Arab, European, American—performed here. In addition, the Lebanese put on elaborate pageants, usually about history and folklore, like the story of Fakhr-ed-Deen.

Before the civil war, exciting events like this ballet were held in the dramatic setting of a Roman temple at Baalbek.

Although there has been little celebration in Lebanon in recent years, the many festivals and holy days have always added much to the life of the Lebanese. Now some of the major celebrations, such as Ramadan and the Christmas season, are once again becoming times for rejoicing. Perhaps revival of other traditional customs and holidays will help the Lebanese people enjoy and take pride in their national heritage, in all its variety.

Like children everywhere, Lebanese kids love a good story.

6. Tall Tales, Short Sayings, Old Beliefs

All over the Arab world, people tell stories about Jeha the fool. (Sometimes he's not so foolish!) Here's a favorite story from Lebanon:

> Jeha, tired of lending his donkey, decided not to let his lazy neighbor Sameer borrow the animal anymore. And sure enough, Sameer did come around, wanting to borrow the donkey again.
>
> "Sorry, but I don't have my donkey," said Jeha.
>
> "Please, Jeha, just this once."
>
> "Impossible. The donkey is not at home."
>
> "Be a good neighbor, Jeha," said Sameer. "I'll return him soon."
>
> "I tell you, my donkey is not here!"
>
> Just then, the donkey, tied in the yard behind Jeha's house, began to bray. "Awwwww! Ee-awwwwwww! Ee-awwww!"
>
> "You lied!" said Sameer. "Your donkey is here!"
>
> Jeha was indignant. "What?" he exclaimed. "You take my donkey's word instead of mine?"

Still More Donkey Trouble

In another story, Jeha finds that more donkeys just mean more trouble.

One day Jeha was hired to take 12 donkeys to market
to sell. It was a long way, so he rode on one. After a
while he counted them to make sure they were all
there. But looking around him, he saw only 11. One
was missing! He got down and walked around to
count them again, tapping each donkey on the nose.
This time there were 12. Relieved, he got back on his
donkey and continued on his way.

Soon he stopped and counted them again—and
again there were only 11. But when he got down and
went around tapping each donkey's nose, he found
12 once more. With a shake of his head, he started
walking beside the donkeys. "Better to walk," he
sighed, "than to keep losing a donkey!"

Whenever Lebanese people get together to enjoy
themselves, they love to tell anecdotes and jokes. Here's a
story about the famous ruler Ameer Basheer, in which a clever
fellow uses his wits to get out of a tight fix:

One day Ameer Basheer's cook served a dish of
eggplant that the ameer found delicious.

"Why, eggplant is a wonderful food," agreed the
cook. "And excellent for your health—your heart,
your liver, everything."

The ameer ate a lot of it. But after a while he
began to feel queasy. He groaned, "Ohhh, it must be
all that eggplant."

"Undoubtedly," answered the cook. "Eggplant

is very hard on the stomach. You should never eat too much—hardly any at all!"

"Now what do you mean by that?" said the ameer. "You just told me that eggplant was good for me!"

"Ah, prince," said the cook. "Am I your servant—or the eggplant's?"

Arabian Stories

The romantic story of Ablah and Antar is another tale that the Lebanese share with their Arab neighbors. Antar, who lived in Arabia in the sixth century, was the son of an Arabian gentleman and a black slave. Though born a slave, he became a heroic warrior and led his tribe in many battles. Finally, he was given his freedom along with the hand of his beloved Ablah, daughter of the chief. Antar was also a poet, whose poems are still read in Arab schools.

His story, based on truth, is still popular today. Folk artists make colorful pictures of Ablah and Antar, often on glass. In the cafés of Tripoli, storytellers used to amuse crowds with tales about Antar. In them, his enemies are always described as very fierce and strong, so that Antar looks even better when he defeats them. The listeners would clap and shout at Antar's victories, and come back the following day to hear what happened next.

The *Arabian Nights* is also part of today's folklore in Lebanon. Children read the adventures of Ali Baba and Sinbad, and books of these stories are favorite gifts at festival times.

Adonis

A legend much older than the Arabian tales is the story of Adonis. Most people know this as a Greek myth, but it really takes place in Lebanon.

Adonis was the most beautiful young man the world had ever seen. Aphrodite, the goddess of love and beauty, fell in love with him, and the two spent happy hours together on the mountainside. Then one day a wild boar killed Adonis. The tears of Aphrodite flowed, and the blood of Adonis stained the earth.

The mountain where Adonis is said to have died rises above the old Phoenician city of Byblos. In ancient times the people of Byblos would mourn the death of Adonis—and then celebrate. Adonis was a symbol of nature, which seems to die in winter but flowers again in spring. The legend says that when Adonis died, the river that flows near Byblos ran red with his blood. Today, every spring, it still runs red . . . for the melting snows and rains carry down red soil from the mountain. And on the mountainside the "blood of Adonis" can still be seen—the bright red anemone flowers that bloom in the spring.

Saint George

Long ago, English knights rode to battle with the cry "For Saint George and England!" Few people today, however, are aware that the patron saint of England, George, lived in Lebanon. The Crusaders learned about him there.

Saint George, the legend says, fought a terrible sea dragon

at the mouth of a river near Beirut. He killed the monster, saving a beautiful princess who had been chained to a rock for the dragon's next meal. The story has been illustrated in paintings for hundreds of years. Saint George is especially important in Orthodox churches.

There is a meaning to the story deeper than simple romance and heroism. Apparently the real George was an early Christian, killed by the Romans. As time went by, people came to believe that this saint had certain powers. He could make water come from dry places, help women bear children, and cure diseases. One ancient shrine to Saint George, near Jouni, is in a cave containing a pool of seawater. Traditionally, women would press pebbles into the hot wax of candles placed by the saint's picture, thinking this would help them to have children. Sick children would be bathed in the pool, in the hope of cure.

Folk Beliefs

Other places are also thought to have miraculous powers. The spot high in the mountains where the Adonis River bursts from a cliff, called Afqa, has long been called holy. The idea goes back to Phoenician times, when people went there to worship the goddess of love. Now a shrine to the Virgin Mary stands next to ruins of a Roman temple to Venus. On a fig tree that branches out over a waterfall near the shrine hang many little rags and pieces of clothing. People put them there in hopes the Virgin will cure an illness, or help a baby to come.

Monasteries where "holy men" are entombed, such as

Saint Sharbel, a 19th-century monk, attract people who hope for a miraculous cure. Often a person promises to do something special if God or a saint cures an illness. A woman may walk on her knees around the church, or a child who has recovered may be dressed in religious gowns for a few years.

Belief in the "evil eye" still lingers in parts of Lebanon, as in other Arab countries. Some people think that an evil spirit, or a person who bears ill will, may wish harm on another person. A person who believes that he or she is attacked in this way may actually suffer and may go to a shrine to ask a saint for help. This is true among both Christians and Muslims. In Muslim communities an important religious man called the sheikh may be able to convince afflicted individuals that they have overcome the evil spirits.

Today even many well-educated Lebanese people may find comfort in what they believe are religious miracles. One instance occurred early in the war. It was said that in a certain part of Beirut the sand in some sandbags was turned to incense, the substance burned in churches to make a pleasing odor. To some people this was a reminder of God's continued love for them in their suffering.

Everyday Expressions

Even in the best of times, people call on God frequently in everyday life. God is called upon to help, comfort, and protect, to permit good things, prevent bad things, and grant wishes. For instance, if you drop your umbrella on a busy street, somebody may say, "*Allah!*" The idea is, may God

Afqa, the source of the Adonis River

prevent an accident, whether big or small, from bringing misfortune. (*Allah* is simply the Arabic word for "God," used equally by Christians and Muslims.)

It is common to say "*inshallah*" often, meaning, "if God wills." For example, "I'll see you tomorrow, *inshallah*." At every greeting, one person says, "How are you?" and the other answers, "Fine, *hamdillah* [praise be to God]." Some people call on God whenever they see something good, whether a new baby or a fine orchard, to ward off the evil eye. Religious people believe that whatever God does is for the best, whether they understand it or not.

A Proverb for Everything

Also, in everyday life, the Lebanese use many proverbs. Some years ago a professor collected well-known sayings—and found more than 4,000 in one small village alone! Many Lebanese proverbs show the importance of the family and neighbors.

> He who takes his clothes off will feel the cold. (If you disregard your family, it's you who will suffer, not they.)

> Your relative, if he chews you, will never spit you out.

Some proverbs are about the importance of education.

> Better blind eyes than a closed mind.

> Seek knowledge even in China.

> Education is worth more to a man than his gold.

But gold is also important to the Lebanese!

> He who has money can eat ice cream in hell.

Many proverbs give a funny view of life, with its senseless ups and downs.

> God gives walnuts to those who have no teeth.

> Throw him in the sea, and he comes up with a fish in his mouth. (A person can profit even in a bad situation.)

> The one who took the donkey up to the roof should

be the one who brings it down. (A person must pay for his or her own foolishness.)

The Love of Language

The Arabs have always been very proud of their language. They love the sounds and rhythms, and the subtle differences in words' meanings. Moreover, Arabic language is an important part of religion, particularly Islam. The Muslims' holy book, the Koran, was first set down in Arabic. Many Muslims, even young children, memorize as much of the Koran as they can.

Poetry is extremely popular, as it has been since ancient times in the Middle East. Young and old, people like to write poetry and to hear poetry recited. A public reading by a good poet will have a standing-room-only crowd.

People also like to curse and threaten in a way that often sounds worse than what is really meant. One interesting result of the recent war was the appearance of political slogans, curses, and poems painted on walls everywhere in public. This "graffiti war" was even described as a new kind of popular literature.

Among educated people who have adopted Western ways, folk sayings and old beliefs are dying out. Many young people have little interest in folktales and customs. They want to be very modern in their ideas, and their tastes are much like those of European and American youth. But the love of talking and of beautiful language is as strong as ever. It is hard to imagine a Lebanese person's day going by without jokes, proverbs, and frequent expressions of the name of God.

A science student at the American University of Beirut

7. *School Is the Rule in Lebanon*

For young people in Lebanon, getting ahead means going to school. Education is one of the biggest enterprises in the country—and a serious business for students.

Lebanon's progress owes a lot to its high level of education. Schooling is compulsory for five years, and normally, almost all children are enrolled in elementary school. About 75 to 80 percent of adults can read and write, a very high percentage compared to most countries of Asia and Africa.

The story of how Lebanon got its head start in schooling goes back to the time when Maronite Christians formed links with the Catholic church in Rome. In 1585 a special school was established in Rome for young Maronite men to study religion and become priests for their people. A little later the ruler Fakhr-ed-Deen allowed European Catholic missionaries to settle in Lebanon. Some of the Maronites trained in Rome began a few schools in Mount Lebanon in the 17th and 18th centuries, though none lasted long. In 1788 a monastery was transformed into a secondary school that taught nonreligious subjects, which set an example for others. Gradually more and more Christians became aware of the need for education.

American Missionaries Start Schools

Under Ameer Basheer's rule, American missionaries from the Presbyterian and Congregational churches were allowed to come to Lebanon in the 1820s and 1830s. They realized that any effort to change people's religions would not get far, so they offered schooling. Although some Christians resented this intrusion by foreign Protestants, others were very ready for modern education. And not only for boys. About 40 girls went to a school that was opened in 1834 by the wife of an American missionary, and the next year a school was started for Druze girls. These were probably the first schools ever offered to girls in that part of the world.

The Americans were followed very shortly by French Catholic missionaries, who eagerly competed with them in the same enterprise. There is a story about a hardworking American missionary who set out from Beirut one morning, telling a friend, "I'm going up to the mountains today to start two schools."

"*Two* schools?" echoed the friend in surprise.

"Yes. I shall get one going—and then the French priest will come along right behind me and start another."

The rivalry soon reached college-level education. In 1866 the Syrian Protestant College was founded in Beirut, on a rocky height overlooking the sea. This school, later renamed the American University of Beirut, has stood on that beautiful site ever since. Not to be outdone, nine years after its founding the French Jesuits started the University of Saint Joseph in downtown Beirut. The French university catered primarily to the Christians, while the American one aimed at making higher education available to anyone.

Throughout the 19th century, schools kept growing in number, some started by foreigners—usually with a religious connection—and the rest by Lebanese people. In 1887 there were 102 schools in the country, reaching about 15,000 students. The majority of students were Christians, because they were more willing to accept the modern education offered by Christian countries of the West. Muslims in general were less inclined, because of the traditional view that all knowledge of value was contained in the religion of Islam.

Yet some 2,500 of the 15,000 students at that time were Muslim. Some Sunni Muslims were becoming very aware of the need for modern education in a world that was starting to change rapidly. To meet this need, a small group in Beirut started a Muslim organization called the Makaased in 1878. In one year they opened four schools, which taught about 940 children. Of these, almost 400 were girls—a remarkable fact, because in traditional Muslim countries girls were not educated at all. Ever since that time, the Makaased Society schools in Beirut and other parts of the country have provided modern education that meets the particular religious needs of Muslims.

By the end of the 19th century, almost any child in Mount Lebanon and the cities could get a primary school education. Good secondary schools and colleges were available for those who could afford them. The only people who were not reached by education were those who lived in distant parts of the country, especially the Shiite Muslims.

The Three Rs in Lebanon

The French Mandate, starting in 1920, put strong emphasis on French language and education. A national system of education was set up that followed the French model—and still does today. Under this system the government decides what will be taught at all schools, whether private or public. Students have nine years of primary and intermediate education, at the end of which they take an examination. Those who go on to secondary school have three more years, then take a major examination called the baccalaureate. If they wish to attend a college or university in Lebanon, they must study for another year and take the second part of the baccalaureate.

Students have no choice as to what subjects they study. They are all required to take math, science, history, geography, Arabic, and often both English and French. Schools offer little in the way of "fun" courses such as art and music, or practical courses in home economics and shop. Some have physical education, and those with enough outdoor room for playing fields have teams in basketball, volleyball, soccer, and track. Most city schools, however, have little room for outdoor exercise.

In normal times, discipline is strict in Lebanese schools. Students expect this—and are quick to "act up" if a teacher is not firm enough. But good students know they have to take their school days very seriously because the examinations are so important and difficult. They feel they have to memorize their lessons so they can write a lot on the exams. Everyone waits in painful suspense for the announcements about who passed and who failed the much-dreaded baccalaureate.

In spite of the requirements set by the government, schooling in Lebanon is as divided as the population. Some people feel, in fact, that it aggravates the divisions among the people. Actually, there are two systems of education: the private schools, and the public schools, which were started by the government in the 1920s.

Private Schools

Private schools differ greatly among themselves. Some are run by various religious groups—Catholic, Muslim, Protestant, Orthodox. There are foreign schools teaching in French, English, Italian, and German, and also Armenian ones. Two prominent schools are American: the American Community School, for grades kindergarten through high school, and a secondary school called International College. Because all American families left during the war, in the 1980s and early 1990s the students at the American Community School were mostly Lebanese and, due to the population changes in Beirut, largely Shiite Muslim.

Many private schools are business enterprises, run to make a profit. In mountain towns and villages, a fee-charging school may be run by a committee from the local people. There are a few specialized private schools, such as one in Beirut for mentally retarded children, started during the war years by the Association of Friends of the Handicapped. Most of the students there are from poor families, so the school depends on donations—yet it managed to send a team to the Special Olympics in Minneapolis, Minnesota, in July 1991.

Choosing schools is a major project for families, for there are many different ones to choose from. Some are very hard to get into and usually take only students whose relatives have been to that school, or who have "pull."

Sometimes, for one reason or another, a child has to change schools several times. This means that he or she may miss certain subjects and likely fall a year or two behind. It's doubly difficult when a child transfers from a school that teaches in one language to a school that teaches in another, yet this happens quite often.

Even young children face a long school day: from eight in the morning till about five in the afternoon. Private schools usually require uniforms and have their own buses, because in normal times the students come from a wide area. Most schools, private and public, used to be either for girls or for boys. This changed during the war, when many schools needed more students.

French or English?

The main division among the private schools is between the French-language and the English-language types. Many Lebanese, especially Christians, attend French-language schools and grow up speaking French, admiring French culture, and feeling more inclined toward Europe than toward the Arab world. Some Muslims also choose these schools because of their high standard of education.

On the other hand, many other Christians and most Muslims and Druze prefer the English-language schools. They learn English and, with more emphasis on their Arab heritage, often acquire different interests and ideas about their country. Formerly, schools of all sorts were attended by students of all faiths. Because of population changes during the war, however, schools became much more segregated by religious group.

Regardless of what private school a child attends, education costs a lot—and the parents must pay. Fees are high, and books have to be bought as well. Educating several children can be a very heavy burden. But families expect this expense. Among the Lebanese, education is one of the most important values. Besides, they feel that good schooling will pay off later when the young man or woman is started in a good job or career. Families will therefore make big sacrifices to keep their children in school as long as possible.

This is true of all the different groups in Lebanon. Villagers who cannot read or write want their sons—and their daughters— to have schooling. Very few young people are allowed to drop out because of rebelliousness or the wish to be independent.

Public Schools

What about the public schools, run by the national government? These schools, which are free except for books, generally serve the rural areas, villages with no private schools, and the poorer people in the cities. Many, however, have had the reputation of being inferior in teaching and equipment.

For a while there was hope that this situation might change. New programs for teacher training were started in the late 1960s, and requirements for teachers in public schools were set higher than those for the private schools. Soon even public schools in poor rural areas were turning out some students well prepared for university work. During the war, many students could not reach the private schools they normally attended, so they went to public schools nearer home. This helped improve those schools somewhat. On the whole, however, public schooling suffered badly because of the war. After the early 1980s the government-run system broke down. Now the private schools are even more important than they were before the war, both in numbers of students and quality of education.

There is yet a third type of school, which is outside the control of the national government. This is the system of schools run by the United Nations for the Palestinians in the refugee camps. About 33,000 children and teenagers go to 83 of these schools in camps around the country. Their teachers are Palestinian, and the classes emphasize information and ideas about Palestine. Here is yet another division in education—which further divides the people who live in Lebanon.

Higher Education

If a student passes both parts of the tough baccalaureate exam, he or she can go to college. Many of those with English-language education aim for the American University of Beirut, though it is expensive and hard to get into. For generations this university and its medical school have trained some of the most important leaders in Lebanon and other Middle Eastern countries, in all fields. AUB kept going throughout the war, with almost full enrollment of around 5,000.

The usual choice of students with French education is the University of Saint Joseph. There are 16 other schools of higher education, most of them private. The large Lebanese University is run by the national government and is free.

Because Lebanon was divided during the war, branches and even new schools were created for students who could not reach those in Beirut. For example, another American school, Beirut University College (now called Lebanese American University), has a main campus in Beirut and a new branch campus in the north-central part of the country.

A good number of Lebanese students go to Europe and the United States for higher education. Lebanese high-school graduates who come to the United States are usually much better prepared in their studies than are most American students. They have had little experience in other school activities, however, because their studies have taken all their time.

School in Wartime and After

Sixteen years of war severely disrupted the schooling of most of Lebanon's children. With all the moving around that people had to do, children naturally had to change schools a lot. Many lost years of schooling. Many were badly wounded, or suffered emotionally from being caught in battles and witnessing so much killing. And many boys, in their early teens or even younger, dropped out of school to join the various militias.

Schools had to close frequently and for long periods. They were looted, destroyed, or occupied by homeless refugee families. Time after time, the important scholastic examinations

The new branch campus of Beirut University College

had to be postponed or cancelled. As Beirut and the whole country became divided along religious lines, the schools did, too. Students could no longer be classmates and friends with others of different groups.

Teachers could not be properly trained. Like other people, they had to move to different places, with the result that some areas had no teachers while others had too many. Where schools could keep going, discipline and respect for authority tended to break down. Teachers were sometimes threatened by armed students or militia soldiers. After the kidnappings started in 1984, almost all of the remaining foreign teachers left the country, which further hurt the quality of instruction.

The surprising thing is that education did not fall to pieces altogether. Instead, schools kept going and people continued to send their children to school whenever and wherever they could. Now that the country is at peace, most children are back in school.

The school system of Lebanon certainly has strengths. Families have a choice of schools, and many schools offer outstanding education. Yet it's not hard to see why, for years, people have argued about education in Lebanon. Should there be so many different kinds of schools—French, English, religious, nationalist? Partly because of the different schools, young people acquire widely differing ideas about themselves and their country—and this can lead to conflict later on. Some people think they should be part of the West; others think they should be only Arab. The lack of a national type of schooling that offers all young people the same basic view of their country is a big problem in this small nation.

A group of high school students relax at the American Community School in Beirut. Now that the country is at peace, most children have returned to school.

Yet few would argue for a rigid system of education that does not allow for variety and freedom of choice. As Lebanon rebuilds, educational leaders are deeply concerned about the ways in which schooling should be changed. Tomorrow, they feel, it must be better suited to the needs of a united country.

8. When There's Time for Recreation . . .

In Lebanon you really can ski in the mountains and swim in the sea on the same morning . . . if you don't mind chilly water. Only an hour's drive separates ski resorts and beaches.

The most famous ski resort is at the Cedars in the north. The grove of ancient trees nestles right below beautiful peaks covered with deep snow. Modern ski lifts, hotels, and chalets make the Cedars a lively spot all winter and a pleasant place to visit in summer as well. Other ski resorts, closer to Beirut, are also scenic and popular.

All along the coast, sandy beaches alternate with rocky patches. A good stretch of sand just south of Beirut has been completely "built up" as commercially run beaches. During the war, people kept coming to these beaches except when the fighting made it absolutely impossible. Now, however, after years of neglect, the area is run-down and the water not very clean. On the seashore north of Beirut are several resorts with large pools and private chalets. Water sports such as boating and water-skiing have been available for many years.

Beirut itself, even before the war, did not offer much chance for outdoor recreation that everyone could enjoy. City parks were very few and small, because land was not set aside for this purpose during the building boom of the 1960s. Nonetheless, people in Lebanon are increasingly aware of good health and fitness. Most city people are limited to jogging and walking, because of the expense of health centers and private sports clubs. The long, broad walk along the sea near the American University, called the Corniche, is a famous place for strolling and jogging—in fact, probably the only safe place in Beirut, because of traffic.

Team Sports

In the small towns and villages, people go for community sports. Almost every community has sports clubs for its young people, both girls and boys. They organize teams for volleyball, basketball, and soccer. Even though mountain villages do not have much level land, most of them manage to squeeze in a small playing field somewhere for volleyball and even soccer. Competition among teams—village, school, and city—is keen. Before the population became divided by war, the city teams and clubs were a mixture of Muslims, Christians, and Druze.

Some business organizations sponsor sports programs. The electricity company at Jouni, for example, has popular basketball teams known as the Kahrubah--meaning simply "electricity."

In the 1960s the national government gave attention to sports and activities for young people. A Department for Youth and Sports was started, aimed at encouraging sports programs all over the country and especially in the villages. After this, the government could not do much more because political problems grew worse. Nevertheless, the teams, clubs, and competitions have continued wherever and whenever possible.

A sport that appeals to boys and young men, now that

peace has returned, is cross-country running in the mountains. Those steep slopes make for tough training! Most people, however, seem to prefer their cars to their feet. Though the mountains are wonderful for long walks, the Lebanese are not a nation of hikers.

There is another outdoor pastime that involves tramping in the countryside: shooting birds. As in other Mediterranean countries, some people shoot birds to eat—but, unfortunately, others shoot just for the fun of it. On the whole, the Lebanese are not fond of animals the way people are in the United States and Europe. The local cats are half wild and rarely make gentle companions. Dogs, though sometimes kept for hunting or as outdoor pets, are usually looked down upon in Arab countries. Not many Lebanese children have the fun of growing up with pets or becoming familiar with different kinds of animals.

When village children play outdoor games, therefore, they don't often have a dog running around with them. But they do have some good games. Like kids everywhere, they play hide-and-seek. The tree-filled terraces and houses built on steep slopes offer many places to hide.

Relaxing at Home

Indoors, board games are always popular. Monopoly—the game of buying and selling real estate—is a favorite. Then there's *tawleh*, which means "table" and is the Arabic name for backgammon. As soon as the men come home from work, out comes a *tawleh* board made of inlaid wood in beautiful patterns. Games of chess, checkers, and cards may go on from

Team sports, like this soccer match, are popular in Lebanon.

late afternoon through the evening, along with much laughing, shouting, and arguing.

A number of indoor games can be played with objects found around the house or with wits alone. Sometimes, like the Phoenicians, children play a word game in which they "send a ship on a long journey." The objects in the cargo all have to start with a certain letter. Anyone who can't think of a good item has to pay a forfeit.

With television in most homes, however, children play these games much less often than before. The Lebanese people seem to be devoted to television. There are more television sets and radios in Lebanon, for the population, than in almost any other country of Asia and Africa. And there is plenty of television to watch. During the war, many of the different armies and militias started their own stations to reach their supporters and to give their own versions of the news. Today, no longer controlled by military groups, certain stations present very good programs.

The Lebanese have a national folk dance called the *debki*, which they do at parties and picnics, festivals and village weddings. Several people in a line, holding hands, step and stamp to the beat of the *derbekki*, a small drum. It's a simple dance but rhythmic and fun. The traditional type of dancing that involves a lot of wiggling of the torso and is often called "belly dancing" is usually seen at nightclubs. Some Lebanese girls belly-dance among their friends. Most young people like the same dances and popular music as Europeans and Americans.

What's the all-time favorite form of recreation in Lebanon?

Sitting and talking. Whether the subject is politics, relatives, food, or Jeha jokes, talking is the great national pastime.

Youth Organizations

There are some organizations for young people that have made an important contribution to the country. Scouting, for boys and girls, has long been popular in Lebanon. When Scout teams compete in sports events, they are frequently said to have the best spirit. Usually Scout groups are connected with schools, though they may be privately run. Many are part of the international Scout program.

Two of the most interesting projects for youth, however, had their start in the war. One is the Red Cross Auxiliary, made up of volunteers—young men and women about 18 to 22 years of age—trained in first aid. During the intense combat in the last years of war, they helped wherever needed, often driving wounded and sick persons from battle zones to hospitals. Doctors came to depend on these young people in saving lives. Moreover, all the fighting forces respected them. They could get through roadblocks where no one else could.

The other important youth program is the summer camps organized by UNICEF, the United Nations organization that helps children. Thousands of children grew up during the war without ever knowing peace or even having a chance to play. In cities and refugee camps under fire, they played nothing but the "game" of war, with death and destruction all around them.

Now there is something that gives these youngsters the fun they need. Starting in 1989, when the fighting was still

Children from all parts of the country get to know one another at a UNICEF camp.

fierce, UNICEF has organized camps every summer. The camps are held all over the country, usually at schools. Each camp offers about 60 girls and boys two weeks of sports, crafts, dancing, hikes, and day trips to different places. The children also learn about the importance of protecting the natural environment. Tens of thousands of children have already gone to the camps—and for many, this is the first fun they have had in their lives.

There's another purpose to these "Education for Peace" camps, and it is just as important. During the war, the country became so divided that people associated only with members of their own religious group. Therefore, each camp is organized so as to bring together children of all classes, all sectarian groups, and all parts of the country, including Palestinians from the refugee camps. They learn to know and like one another. They also learn about their country and take pride in being Lebanese, rather than just members of particular groups.

The camp counselors, several thousand specially trained young people aged 18 to 24, also come from all parts of the Lebanese and Palestinian population. Some of the young men were formerly in militias and fought against one another. They, too, are learning to know one another as individuals, rather than as members of an enemy group.

The UNICEF camps are bringing happiness to the lives of Lebanese children—and helping to mold stronger future citizens. This effort, along with plans to make more parks and recreational opportunities available for everyone, may lead to a healthier Lebanon tomorrow.

9. The Lebanese in America

Lebanon has always been a crossroads, a place where people meet, where people come and go. The cliffs above the Dog River bear a record of one type of visitor to Lebanon—the many historical conquerors who carved their "calling cards" on the rocks.

Other people went to Lebanon for different reasons, and remained. Lebanon has served as a haven for groups who could not stay in their own country. The Maronite Christians found a safe home in the high mountains long ago. In this century, the Armenians and the Palestinians sought refuge in Lebanon because they had to leave their own countries. Other outsiders were attracted because life was good in Mount Lebanon. This happened in Roman times and when Fakhr-ed-Deen and Ameer Basheer ruled the land.

But people have always been leaving Lebanon, too. Phoenician traders and explorers sailed forth, as did merchants in later times. In the 1870s and 1880s, people began to leave Lebanon again. Why did they wish to go?

There was peace, but problems persisted. As the population in the mountains grew larger, the amount of land each family could farm grew smaller. Many found it harder and harder to make a living. The Turkish overlords who ruled the whole area were resented and feared. Memories of the massacre in 1860 lingered. But people were not *forced* to leave. Rather, they wanted better chances in life. They were ambitious and wanted to see the world.

Fortunately, large parts of the world were opening up at that time, ready for people willing to work hard and win the rewards. North America, Latin America, Africa, and Australia all beckoned. They offered what the ambitious Lebanese could never hope for in the old country. Soon, in an explosion of emigration, the Lebanese were leaving their homeland and traveling all over the world.

The Early Adventurers

In 1876 the Arabs "discovered" America. The very first were a few merchants from Jerusalem and probably Beirut, who went to the Centennial Exposition in Philadelphia. They soon found that Americans were happy to buy goods, such as pearl jewelry, decorative objects carved from olive wood, silks, and embroideries, from the Holy Land. They brought back glowing tales of their profits.

The word spread fast that anyone could become wealthy in America, and the people of Mount Lebanon listened eagerly. Adventurous young men started to leave for the land of opportunity, eager to make their fortunes. They traveled as individuals, not in organized groups, and many were penniless. Their families and friends had to scrape together money for the cheapest boat passage.

Once they had arrived in the United States, some settled in eastern cities such as Boston and New York. But unlike many other immigrants with no money, they did not care to work in factories. If they did take such work, they were determined to move on to something better as quickly as possible. Farming did not interest them much, either; only a very few took advantage of the land available in the Midwest.

Then what *did* these poor newcomers do? They walked for a living. The Lebanese wanted freedom and independence, so they became peddlers. Usually helped by someone who had come a few years earlier, they would make up a pack of small, inexpensive items and set out on foot. They walked from house to house, town to town, state to state, even from one part of the country to another. After a while, peddling "networks" grew up in various places to help the latest arrivals.

People in rural areas, who could not get to stores easily, were delighted to see the Lebanese peddler come along with goods both practical and pretty . . . shoelaces, knives, cloth, tools, inexpensive jewelry. The Lebanese made themselves useful and noticeable from the start.

Not only men and boys became peddlers. Many a Lebanese woman set out on her own and peddled her way around the United States. A few even left husband and children back in the old country and sent money home from their earnings. These were brave and enterprising women indeed.

Getting Ahead in America

By going out to meet the Americans, the peddlers got to know the country and the people quickly, and they also learned English. Along with their sturdy feet, they had good heads for business. By the early 1900s some were earning as much

The Lebanese peddler became a familiar figure to rural Americans in the 19th century.

as five dollars a day—an astonishing amount in those days. Meanwhile, they lived very simply, denying themselves all comforts, and saved every penny they could. Their hard work paid off. Typically, Lebanese peddlers would first buy a horse and wagon, then settle down to start a shop—or whatever respectable work they thought would make money. Relatives and persons from the same village or the same religious sect would help one another get started.

A good number did very well indeed. Even before World War I, fortunes were being made by Lebanese immigrants from Massachusetts to California. They sold Oriental rugs and silk garments; they manufactured clothes, ran restaurants and grocery stores, carried on banking. By 1908 a directory of Arab-American businesses in the United States included at least one in every state. This is all the more remarkable considering the very small land they came from, with a population of a few hundred thousand.

The early immigrants were almost all Christians, especially Christians from the mountains. Just as they had been eager to accept modern education offered by Christian countries of Europe and America, they were eager to go to those countries. Most Muslims, on the other hand, disliked the idea of going to a Christian nation, where there were no mosques. They feared it would not be comfortable for them there and they would lose their religion.

Gradually, however, Muslims and Druze did start coming to the United States. In fact, as early as 1907 a society was formed by young Druze men in Seattle, Washington. Early in the 1920s Lebanese Muslims headed for Detroit, attracted by

Many early Lebanese immigrants worked hard to set up small businesses, like this grocery story in Birmingham, Alabama.

good wages in the automobile industry. Unlike the Christians, they were not eager to fit into American society. Rather, they wanted to keep separate so they could support one another in their religion. Therefore, these Muslims, largely Shiite, preferred the settled life of factory work, rather than peddling.

Soon mosques were built in Michigan, Indiana, and Iowa. Well-organized Lebanese Muslim communities have lived in Detroit and Dearborn, Michigan, and in Toledo, Ohio, for many years.

For the first few decades of Lebanese immigration, no one thought of these people as Lebanese. Instead, they were called Syrian, because the whole area of the Middle East that included Mount Lebanon was then called Syria. Sometimes they were even described as Turks, because Turkey governed the Middle East at that time. Only in the 1920s, after the formation of the modern state of Lebanon, did the term Lebanese start to become common.

As for individual Lebanese, many kept their Arabic names. Others, for convenience and "Americanization," changed to new names that had the same meaning in English, or a similar sound. Thus the common name Haddad often became the even more common name Smith, which is what it means. Dark-eyed, olive-skinned Americans with the English names of Thomas, Sawyer, Small, George, or Peters were once called Tuma, Sawaya, Sagheer, Girgus, or Boutros.

Settling Down

Early Lebanese newcomers to America usually planned to return to their home villages after saving enough money. But the first decades of the 20th century brought political troubles to Lebanon—and in the meantime, life was very good in the United States. Therefore, most immigrants decided to buy property and settle down. Often a man would work until he was fairly well-off, then return to his village, find a bride, and bring her back. Whenever immigrants had the money, they would bring other members of their families to join them. They settled in towns and cities all over the United States.

Elementary school children at an Arab school in Birmingham, Alabama, in the 1920s

Young people were expected to help their families, but their parents also tried to give them as many advantages as possible, especially education.

Once they had settled down, Lebanese immigrant families and communities stuck together closely and made sure that their members behaved well. Family honor was still very

important. In the cities and towns where they lived, these new Americans were known from the start as good citizens, hardworking and law-abiding. Many communities built their own churches and were further strengthened by frequent visiting among relatives and neighbors, the custom so important in the old country.

No matter how good their lives in the new country, the immigrants never forgot their families and villages back in Lebanon. Whenever possible, they sent home money. From the 1880s on, nearly every Lebanese village began to improve. Thanks to the hard work and loyalty of the sons and daughters who had gone abroad, families could build fine stone houses with orange-tiled roofs, buy more land, construct better terraces. Villages and towns acquired new school buildings, churches, and hospitals. Thus the Lebanese in America got ahead very nicely, and also helped their mother country grow stronger.

Besides being good citizens, what have the Lebanese done for America? Anyone who lives in a town with a Lebanese community can think of a ready answer. They start restaurants. A good Lebanese restaurant will probably be one of the most popular eating places in town.

In fact, Americans may owe that very American delight, the ice-cream cone, to the quick thinking of a Lebanese immigrant. At the St. Louis World's Fair in 1904, it is said, an ice-cream seller ran out of little plates. Next to him was a Lebanese man selling freshly made waffles. Noticing his neighbor's problem, the Lebanese man deftly shaped a warm waffle into a cone. Instant success!

Some Successful and Well-Known Lebanese-Americans

While the Lebanese have contributed in all sorts of fields, entertainment is certainly one of the most noticeable. The actor Danny Thomas not only had a star career on television—he founded and organized support for St. Jude Hospital in Memphis, Tennessee, which carries on treatment and research in severe diseases affecting children. His daughter Marlo Thomas, actress and promoter of social causes, and his son Tony Thomas, producer, are also well known in television.

The late Danny Thomas on a visit to St. Jude Hospital in Memphis, Tennessee.

Other actors are Jamie Farr (*M*A*S*H*), F. Murray Abraham (*Amadeus*), Michael Nouri (*Flashdance*), Kathy Najimy (*Sister Act*), and Vic Tayback (TV series *Alice*). Writers William Blatty (*The Exorcist*) and Callie Khouri (*Thelma & Louise*) have won Oscars, as did set decorator Emile Kuri for two outstanding films of the 1950s.

Well-known personalities in popular music are Casey Kasem, host of major TV and radio music shows such as *American Top 40*, and singer-songwriter Paul Anka. Classical musicians include Rosalind Elias, a famous opera singer.

Casey Kasem, host of pop music shows

In literature an outstanding name is Kahlil Gibran, one of several Lebanese poets and writers who lived in New York and Boston early in the 20th century. Gibran's book *The Prophet*, published in 1923, is still widely read today. His cousin and godson, also named Kahlil Gibran, is a sculptor and inventive artist in Boston.

Lebanese-American professors are found in major universities and colleges all over the country. Lebanese-American doctors and scientists have made important advances. Dr. Michael De Bakey did pioneering work in heart surgery at Baylor University School of Medicine in Houston, Texas. In 1990 the Nobel Prize for Chemistry went to Dr. Elias Corey at Harvard University.

Public affairs is another area where Lebanese-Americans contribute significantly to this country. Ralph Nader is doubtless the best-known activist anywhere for consumer and citizen rights. Helen Thomas, United Press International correspondent, has appeared prominently at White House press conferences under the last seven presidents. Dr. Donna Shalala was appointed secretary of health and human services in President Bill Clinton's cabinet; formerly she was the president of Hunter College and chancellor of the University of Wisconsin. Philip Habib, a career diplomat, became well known in negotiations concerning the war in Lebanon.

In addition to having representatives in both houses of the U.S. Congress, Lebanese-Americans are increasingly active in politics at all levels. The Senate majority leader in the early 1990s is a Lebanese-American, Senator George Mitchell of Maine.

Dr. Donna Shalala was appointed to the cabinet by President Bill Clinton

As for the business world, Lebanese-American women and men excel in such fields as banking, investment, technology, construction, manufacturing, real estate, and travel. A great many Americans wear a Lebanese name on their pants: Both Haggar and Farah pants are made by firms started many years ago by Lebanese entrepreneurs in Texas.

Among athletes with Lebanese-American backgrounds, Doug Flutie of Boston College won the highest collegiate football award, the Heisman Trophy, in 1984. Abe Gibron and Bill George also had outstanding careers in professional football. Winner of the 1986 Indianapolis 500 auto race was Bobby Rahal.

For the Lebanese, the United States has certainly been the land of opportunity—and they have made the most of it.

Lebanese-American Organizations

In the past, some Lebanese communities tended so well to their business that they kept themselves rather separate from

American society and even from other Arab groups. Now Lebanese-Americans are broadening their concerns. They have founded and taken leadership roles in various Arab-American organizations focused on public affairs, such as the National Association of Arab Americans. Another is the Arab American Institute in Washington, D.C., which encourages participation by Arab-Americans in politics. The American-Arab Anti-Discrimination Committee promotes awareness of civil rights issues, especially those affecting the Arab-American community.

The war in Lebanon produced several new organizations active in the United States. The organization Save Lebanon helps war victims, especially children, from all groups and all parts of the country. The American Task Force for Lebanon encourages good relations between the U.S. and Lebanon, and works toward long-range solutions to Lebanon's problems.

The war also produced a new wave of Lebanese immigrants to this country. These were not poor people seeking to get ahead for the first time. Rather, they were largely students and well-educated persons who left home in order to get on with their studies or careers. Many students have been helped by the Hariri Foundation. Rafiq al-Hariri, a wealthy self-made businessman, also supports various projects in Lebanon such as reconstruction plans for Beirut—and was appointed prime minister of Lebanon in 1992.

The recent Lebanese immigrants can doubtless contribute a lot to the United States. But they are also the sort of people whom Lebanon needs. Will they take their skills and ambition back to their homeland? For a long time their prospects in

Lebanon looked bleak. Now, however, their country appears to be on the threshold to a much better future. If Lebanon's leaders are wise, they will see that educated, capable persons are welcomed back and put to work to help the country mend and grow.

Surely a country with such a long and distinctive history, one that has made valuable contributions in so many ways, will prosper once again in the future. In spite of all its troubles, this tiny land has earned a large place in our world today.

Appendix A:

Embassies and Consulates of Lebanon in North America

United States:

Embassy of Lebanon
2560 28th Street, NW
Washington, D.C. 20008
(202) 939-6300

Consulate of Lebanon
9 East 76th Street
New York, New York 10021
(212) 744-7905/6

Consulate of Lebanon
7060 Hollywood Boulevard, Suite 510
Hollywood, California 90028
(213) 467-1253/4

Consulate of Lebanon
1959 East Jefferson, Suite 4A
Detroit, Michigan 48207
(313) 567-9233/4

Canada:

Embassy of Lebanon
640 Lyon Street
Ottawa, Ontario K1S 3Z5
(613) 236-5825

Consulate of Lebanon
40, Chemin Cote Ste Catherine
Montreal, Quebec H2V 2A2
(514) 276-2638

Appendix B:

A Note on Language

Arabic, the native language of Lebanon, is written in an alphabet completely different from the Roman letters used for English and other European languages. The Arabic alphabet and language are ancient and are related to other Semitic languages such as Hebrew.

Most of the 29 letters have at least two different forms. The form used depends on the place where the letter appears in the word. Here are some of the letters.

Name of Letter	Form of Letter by Itself	Beginning of Word	Middle	End	Sound
Ba	ب	بـ	ـبـ	ـب	B
Ta	ت	تـ	ـتـ	ـت	T
Dal	د	د	ـد	ـد	D
Fa	ف	فـ	ـفـ	ـف	F
Kaf	ك	كـ	ـكـ	ـك	K
Meem	م	مـ	ـمـ	ـم	M

Many of the vowel sounds are not written. The reader has to recognize the word to know how it should be pronounced— or else make a good guess!

Arabic is written from right to left. Books and newspapers are read from back to front—or so it looks to English speakers. At first, learning Arabic is quite a challenge for someone from a non-Arab country. But soon the learner can get used to the new letters and way of writing, and it seems more natural.

Because the alphabet is so different, Arabic words have to be transliterated when written in English or other European languages. This means they are spelled in a way to sound like the Arabic pronunciation. There are, however, different systems for doing this; therefore, words can be spelled in various ways. For instance, the Bekaa Valley can also be spelled *Biqa'* or *Beqaa* or *Bekaa'*. In this book a simple method is used in hopes that readers can pronounce the words with ease.

Spoken Arabic, called colloquial, sounds somewhat different from written Arabic. Moreover, the several Arab countries pronounce many words differently. On radio and TV, people usually speak what is called modern standard Arabic, because that form is understood in all the Arab countries.

Arabic has given many familiar words to English and other European languages. Here are a few: admiral (*ameer*, ruler); algebra (*al jabar*, reduction); candy (*qandi*, cane sugar); chemistry (*al keemiya*, alchemy); coffee (*qahwi*); cotton (*qutn*); jar (*jarra*); lemon (*laymoon*); racket for tennis (*rahah*, palm of the hand); rice (*riz*); and sugar (*sookkar*). Though Arabic has a very large vocabulary, it

also adopts many modern words from other languages.
The numerals used in Arabic are written as follows:

0—٠	4—٤	8—٨	15—١٥
1—١	5—٥	9—٩	20—٢٠
2—٢	6—٦	10—١٠	50—٥٠
3—٣	7—٧	11—١١	100—١٠٠

The numbers that we use (in contrast to Roman numerals)
are derived from these and are called Arabic numerals. It is
said that the Arabs, a thousand years ago or more, first
discovered the importance of the zero and the decimal point,
which made possible major advances in mathema-
tics, science, and technology.

Selected Bibliography

Cobban, Helena. *The Making of Modern Lebanon.* Boulder, Colo.: Westview Press, 1985.

Friedman, Thomas L. *From Beirut to Jerusalem.* New York: Farrar, Straus & Giroux, 1989.

Gordon, David C. *The Republic of Lebanon: Nation in Jeopardy.* Boulder, Colo.: Westview Press, 1983.

Hitti, Philip K. *Lebanon in History: From the Earliest Times to the Present.* 3rd ed. London: Macmillan, 1967.

Naff, Alixa. *Becoming American: The Early Arab Immigrant Experience.* Carbondale: Southern Illinois University Press, 1985.

Salibi, Kamal S. *The Modern History of Lebanon.* New York: Praeger, 1965; Greenwood Press, 1976.

Thubron, Colin. *The Hills of Adonis: A Journey in Lebanon.* Boston: Little, Brown, 1969; New York: Atlantic Monthly Press, 1990.

Books for Younger Readers

Harik, Elsa Marston. *The Lebanese in America.* Minneapolis: Lerner Publications, 1987.

Heide, Florence Parry, and Judith Heide Gilliland. *Sami and the Time of the Troubles.* New York: Clarion, 1992.

Shapiro, William E. *Lebanon.* New York: Franklin Watts, 1984.

Index

Islam, 28-29, 35, 37-38, 67, 68, 83, 87
Israel, 7, 15, 29, 44, 45, 46, 47, 51

Jeita Cave, 12
Jouni, 13, 79, 98

Koran, 67, 83

language, 18-19, 23-24, 83, 90
Litani, 12

Makaased Society, 87
Maronites, 27, 30, 38, 40, 42, 43, 45, 85, 106
marriages, 53, 56, 57
militias, 47, 93, 95, 102
missionaries, 41, 69, 85, 86
money, 49, 57, 69, 82, 114
Mount Lebanon, 7, 16, 38, 40, 41, 42, 43, 72, 85, 87, 106, 107, 112
music, 19, 70, 72, 102
Muslims, 14, 18, 26, 27, 28-30, 31, 38, 39, 42, 45, 46, 55, 57, 66, 67, 68, 81, 83, 87, 90, 98, 110-111

names, 54, 112
New Year, 68, 69

organizations, 19, 119
Orontes River, 12
Ottoman Turks, 40, 41, 42, 43

Palestinians, 29-30, 44-45, 47, 51, 92, 105, 106
peddlers, 108, 110, 111
Phoenicians, 32, 34, 35, 106
poetry, 83
population, 13, 16, 17, 24, 26-27, 31, 35, 48, 49, 89, 91, 98, 102, 106, 110
poverty, 14, 23, 29, 31, 62

private schools, 89-91, 92, 93
proverbs, 81-83
public schools, 91-92

Ramadan, 65, 66, 73
recreation, 97-99, 102-103, 105
Red Cross Auxiliary, 103
reconstruction, 14, 21, 49, 62, 96, 119
refugee camps, 29-30, 92, 103, 105
religious groups, 26-30, 31, 44, 89, 91, 104
restaurants, 14, 114

Saladin, 39
seaports, 13, 14, 22
Shiites, 28-29, 30, 45, 47, 48, 49, 54, 68, 87, 89, 111
shopping, 14, 24, 25, 26, 68
Sidon, 13, 15, 34, 35, 38, 46
sports, 98-99
Sunnis, 28, 29, 30, 87
Syria, 7, 12, 38, 41, 42, 45, 47, 49, 112

Taif Accord, 48
teachers, 41, 91, 95, 117
television, 102, 115, 116
terrorism, 46, 47, 48, 95
trade, 13, 22, 32, 34, 35, 39, 41, 44, 107
transportation, 16, 24, 35, 58, 62
trees, 10, 11, 12
Tripoli, 13, 14, 38, 77
Tyre, 13, 15, 34, 35, 46

UNICEF, 103-105
United States, 44, 46-47, 93, 107-108, 110-119

war, 14, 15, 19, 20, 21, 22, 29, 31, 38, 41, 42, 43, 44, 45-49, 51, 62, 67, 72, 80, 83, 89, 90, 91, 92, 93, 97, 98, 102, 103-105, 110, 117, 119
water sports, 97
women's liberation, 24

About the Author

Elsa Marston, a native of Massachusetts, first went to Lebanon after earning a master's degree in international affairs at Harvard University. Her journey started a lifelong interest in the Middle East and North Africa; she has also lived in Carthage, Tunisia, and Cairo, Egypt. She and her family witnessed the start of the Lebanese civil war in 1975, and went back in 1992 to observe the results of war and prospects for peace. Ms. Marston specializes in multicultural literature, focusing on the Middle East and other Third World countries, and writes both fiction and nonfiction for young people. She lives in Bloomington, Indiana, with her husband, Iliya Harik, a native of Lebanon. One of their three sons was a teacher in Beirut in 1992-1993.